Rogue Journal of Undergraduate Research

Issue 1

Summer 2013

Kyle Kahlil Pate – Managing Editor, Founder

Catherine Bernards – Editor

Preston Price – Editor

Jane Silva – Editor

Support from:

Associated Students of Southern Oregon University

Hannon Library

Southern Oregon University

With special thanks to:

Sue Walsh, Paul Adalian, Jody Waters, Jim Rible, and our anonymous referees.

All work copyright its respective author, 2013. All rights reserved.

Contents

The Promise of the Internet: Boon or Boondoggle?..4

    References..18

A Closer Look at the Early Detection and Prevention of School Shootings..............................22

    Abstract..22

    References..29

Eye Am Watching You: CCTV - The Metal Ring of Hope...31

    Abstract..31

    References..49

    Appendix..51

Twenty-First Century Alice..55

    References..63

The Significance of Porn and its Effect on Committed Relationships with a Focus on Heterosexual Couples and the Female Counterpart..64

    Abstract..64

    References..69

The Promise of the Internet: Boon or Boondoggle?

Public Discourse in the Age of Entertainment Styling

Wendy Temple – Southern Oregon University

Debate concerning the quality of public discourse is an ongoing one with the voices of many contributing. This paper grounds itself in the works of those who have gone before, people such as Neil Postman, Marshall McLuhan, Harold Innis, and Walter Ong. The intent of this paper is to extend the discussion to include the Internet's effects on public discourse. In addition, I would like to add that it is not only technology that shapes society, but society that shapes technology as well. I maintain that the relationship between technology and society is reiterative and recursive, and I frame an illustration of this circular relationship around the Internet's effects on the quality of public discourse and society's effects on the Internet's actuality. In short, I attempt to demonstrate that the Internet affects discourse, but that society determines the Internet's potential, and that determination may not be the Internet's ideal potential.

The adoption of any technology brings with it unique metaphorical extensions and amputations of the human self (1). The extensions are usually celebrated and immediately obvious as they tend toward easing life's physical or mental labors, but the technology that provides these extensions also takes something away, usually something less immediately obvious. The following examples, though condensing the actual history of events, demonstrate McLuhan's idea of metaphorical extensions and amputations. The technology of the automobile offered the medium of driving, an extension of the body, and while that was being celebrated, the body's legs were essentially amputated as the one went from a life centered around walking to one centered around driving, meaning the actual infrastructure became one in which driving was a necessity and walking could seldom, if ever, be the primary mode of transportation. The television offers the entertainment medium of easy to understand visual stories, eliminating the need to read a book, to the point where illiteracy is on the rise. Email offers nearly instant communication, but negates the need for a nicely crafted, handwritten letter, to the point where nary a letter is seen in the mail.

This phenomenon of 'something gained, something lost' could conceivably be argued all the way back to the wheel (1). It also explains the euphoria and the cynicism which greets each new technology. What is interesting to note is that all of the extension's associated amputations were the latent results of societal choices in the amount and manner of technological adoption and media use. The giddiness and euphoria induced by new toys (cars, televisions and computers) caused a pervasive myopia resulting in, and from, technological adoption and media use with little thought about possible repercussions or ramifications. However, walking, reading and writing did not have to be so compromised. With cultural media literacy, media use could be moderated since "no medium is excessively dangerous if its users understand what its dangers are" (2). (Admittedly, the dangers are more readily visible in hindsight.) The amount and manner of technological adoption and media use, then, determines what societal amputations await. This sentiment is, on its surface, wholly of the technological determinist persuasion, but the assertion that it is the manner and extent of technological adoption which determines societal amputations places the relationship between society and technology into one more akin to a feedback loop.

Changes in communication models are heavily laden with ideological consequences, and as such, media, form and content, must be consumed with careful consideration and awareness. The nature of public discourse has already suffered in what Neil Postman dubbed "The Age of Show Business" (3). Television's reliance on *schein*, the appearance of things, as opposed to *sein*, the substance of things (4), is evident in its programming, even news. Television's rise to media primacy during the Age of Show Business (the latter half of the 20th century), and its reliance on *schein*, has undermined public discourse. A more recent development, the Internet, was "welcomed as a powerful global communication tool that was said to open the first truly boundless space of communication" (5). The Internet's realm of participation, not representation, provided the ideal democratic arena, one that could usher in the return of a heightened discursive and reasoning public sphere and emphasize the *sein* of things. Yet, under the same myopia that other technological changes have witnessed, futuristic fervor greeted the Internet, the Internet's possible shortcomings dismissed or ignored. Under the guise of several different aliases, such as the capitalist influences of gatekeeping and customization and user ignorance or apathetic indifference, the Internet has become retrogressive, leading to societal compromise.

The societal compromise is the collective acceptance of the representative public sphere. Understanding the impact of this acceptance requires understanding the differences between representative and reasoning public spheres and understanding the public sphere's place in democracy. While full deliberation on each of these topics is outside the scope of this paper, sentiments from the Age of Reason (roughly 1650 to the early 1800's) provide some clarity. If "we leave the people in ignorance," Thomas Jefferson warned, "kings, priests and nobles…will rise up among us." (6) Further elaborating on Thomas Jefferson's views, Mark Bauerlein states, "Education would preserve the sovereignty of the people, and without it, the very system designed to represent them would descend into yet another tyranny in the dismayingly predictable course of nations" (6). The dissemination and analysis of knowledge, then, is essential to a functioning democracy. Indeed, democracy demands an educated and civically responsible electorate and the fostering and nurturing of a discursive, reasoning public sphere as opposed to a representative public sphere. The "private autonomy of citizens [serves] as the precondition for the realization of popular sovereignty through the use of public reason [in the public sphere]" (7). In a democracy, there are certain 'checks and balances' restricting intra-governmental powers, but it is the public sphere that acts as the weightiest counterbalance to potential tyranny.

The nature of the public sphere dictates the quality of government. The visualization of a scale with government on one side and the public sphere on the other aids understanding here. With weighty civic discourse in the public sphere, the government is 'checked' and rises to its ideal; conversely, with airy and trivial pop-culture discourse of no weight at all, the government is able to sink to its lowest levels of corruption. The nature of the discourse within the public sphere dictates the nature of its sphere. Jürgen Habermas theorized that the reasoning public sphere allows for argument, critique, analysis, investigation, equality, horizontal participation, and an emphasis on the essence of fact (*sein*). The representative public sphere, on the other hand, relies on staging of personality, show, image, aura, top-down rule, and emphasis on the appearance of fact (*schein*) (8). In a reasoning public sphere, the constituents are civically engaged, and the discourse within the sphere is critical and analytical. In a representative public sphere, on the other hand, the constituents are obedient and laudatory or lackadaisical, and the discourse is trivial to civics. The nature of media dictates the discourse within the public sphere. The medium of choice, with its inherent biases toward aura, investigation, image, or fact, affects how opinions are formed and iterated. Marshall McLuhan went so far as to say that the medium is the message. "Societies have always been shaped more by the nature of the media by which men communicate than by the content of the communication" (9). This implies that the societal amputations resulting from the nature and extent of media adoption could include potential transformations in governmental reality.

A look into television's epistemology and the sort of public sphere the medium fosters, coupled with the decline in public discourse and erosion of civil rights during television's reign, serves as a good example of this dynamic. The major exception to the gradual loss of civil rights would seem to be the Civil Rights Movement of the 1960's. Rather than being the first breaths of a new age, however, that movement was merely the last gasps of an age primarily dependent on print media. The gradual loss of civil rights is real, even if shrugged off as not that serious by many Americans, and its reality is made possible by a public more concerned with 'reality shows' or celebrity 'news' than with the erosion of personal freedoms (10). Most recently, the National Defense Authorization Act of 2012, NDAA, signed by President Obama, allows for the indefinite detention of American citizens suspected of terrorist affiliation. While an injunction immediately barred detentions of this nature, the Obama administration is now fighting that injunction and refuses to acknowledge whether it has ever been abided (11). The fight is indicative of the contemporary civil rights climate where the freedom to endlessly consume products and media obscures the reality, the loss of freedom. Also, televised aspects of presidential campaigns over the last few decades mark a trend towards appearances versus substance, and while some commend the increased information provided by observing candidate's non-verbal cues via television (12), a "growing body of research has found print media, particularly newspapers, to be more conducive to active citizenship" (13).

As a visual medium, television frames all discourse through the lens of visual primacy. Thus, for many, to look to television as a conveyor of important cultural conversations is to forget television's epistemology (14). Television, by its nature, appeals to emotions rather than to reason. It is a visual medium not that far removed from photography. A viewer's visceral, emotional reaction to a picture is the reason a picture is "worth a thousand words." Examining the prevalence of first, the "sound bite," and then the "image bite" demonstrates this point. (The sound bite is a short audio/video clip of only a few seconds in length. The image bite is the same, but there is no sound, or someone other than the person in the image is speaking, perhaps a narrator or commentator.) A sound and image bite analysis of televised presidential campaigns from 1992 to 2004 demonstrates the decreasing duration of presidential candidates' sound bites and increasing duration of image bites (12), bringing campaigning ever closer to appearances and slogans and farther from substance. Again, the nature of the television medium subordinates verbal content to visual interest due to what scholars call "visual dominance."

When confronted with visual and aural messages, the brain's visual dominance impairs the memory for verbal information (12). This is particularly true when messages conflict or are emotionally disturbing. With the increased dissonance caused by the confusion between the aural and visual content or the strong emotional reaction to the content, the brain filters the aural message out in favor of the visual message (15). The phenomenon of visual dominance is at the very heart of television's epistemology, and it explains the real difficulty in television's use as a cultural conversationalist of any import. People remember what they see; that is, they remember the emotions attached to the images and do not recall the verbal appeal to the rational mind. For this reason alone, television should not even be a contender for media primacy in a democratic society, a society in which *sein* should have a higher priority than *schein*.

Thus, the societal amputation associated with television is the rational mind. Reasoning is traded away in exchange for emotional thrills and delights, a bargain of Faustian proportion. None of this is to say that television is a malevolent force or that it has no value, but its value is in entertainment, vacuous and otherwise. Indeed, television is most pernicious when it parades itself as a medium of discourse for the discursive public sphere (16). Topics of rational nature should be considered in a medium that allows for rational thought, which tends to be discouraged by presentation in the visual medium of television. The print medium has often been shown to be more conducive to rational study. Hence, television's epistemology limits a television-based culture to a representative public sphere. The tragic return to a representative public sphere is due to the fact that television's predominant use eclipses, and nearly replaces, the use of print media (17).

Habermas described the emergence of the discursive public sphere as being dependent on the emergence of "the critical and universalizing force of publicity that slowly undermine[s] and ultimately replace[s] the old representative order" (5). In other words, as public knowledge, interaction and dissertation increase, a critical mass is reached that changes the nature of the public sphere towards discursive. Where the Age of Reason saw a shift from representative to reasoning public spheres, television culture in the Age of Show Business saw a return to the representative. Timothy Leary's succinct personal development sequence, "Turn on; tune in; drop out," commonly misinterpreted as "Get stoned and abandon all constructive activity" (18), could be co-opted as the Age of Show Business theme: Turn on the tube; tune in to the entertainment; drop out of civic life. However, because Timothy Leary may not appreciate this co-opting, perhaps an even more concise and less verbal theme is in order: Tune in (to the tube); tune out (of civic responsibility).

The question now is, will the Internet cause, or allow, a critical mass to turn on critical thinking, tune into reason, and drop out of entertainment, thus fulfilling the Internet's promise of elevating public discourse and returning argument to its rightful throne, a throne usurped by appearances? Much of the answer lies in looking at Google, the Internet oracle. While the Internet and Google are distinctly separate entities, they are closely intertwined. Google and its many services (Google Chrome, Google Search, Google Mail, Google Maps, Google Earth, Google Analytics, Google Images, Google Translate, Google Directions, Google News and Google+) essentially give the Internet its easy and convenient usability. Also, because Google is the Internet force to be reckoned with and because its lagging competitors have the same capitalist influences and similar, if not quite the same, means, this paper will use Google as an example (19).

In other words, what would Google do? According to Jeff Jarvis, Google gives the people elegantly organized, egalitarian control (20). Indeed, this is precisely what Google appears to do. The Internet sits at the eye of the digital media maelstrom, with every imaginable communications medium swirling around, a mouse click away from being subdued into consumption or production. The information of the world awaits every user: history, music, art, science, mathematics, philosophy. There is no subject not represented in cyberspace. Products may be sold or purchased, employment may be found or offered, universities may be attended, and jobs may be performed all online. The Internet also offers every form of digital entertainment and socializing, from television shows, movies and comedy, to online gaming, email, instant messaging and social networking. At its best, the Internet is wholly democratic, which gives the Internet its greatest potential, the potential to shift towards a reasoning public sphere. Mills, Dewey, Habermas and Hegel all could agree on the concept that a public, or public sphere, is based on "dialogue, debate and conflict," on an unending process of struggle requiring continuous engagement and authentic conversation (21). This understanding of a public suggests that the increased interaction inherently possible in the Internet medium may reinvigorate a critical mass towards critical thinking, resulting in a return to a discursive public sphere. The Internet is undoubtedly the medium of a new age, one in which civic participation can flourish, people can educate themselves in any expertise, and anyone can become somebody.

One theme uniting many proponents for the Internet is Public Relations. Ries & Ries tell of the fall of advertising and the rise of public relations. Their mantra "Advertising reaches everybody; PR reaches somebody" (22) could well become an Internet jingle as, through the selling of users' data, homogenous groups of similar consumers are presented to companies, courtesy of Google. Tracy Cooley adds that the Internet may serve as a means to open communication between businesses and customers (23). Jeff Jarvis lauds Google's business acumen and its new world order, an order based on public relations, albeit public relations according to a Google sense, which stresses listening to customers' opinions and thereby aligning business policies. Cooley acknowledges this as essential to contemporary public relations firms (24). Incidentally, Google-like public relations also includes the customized, niche marketing made possible by Google's users' data. The celebration of the Internet's marketing potential could be summed up with Jarvis's "Google commodifies everything" (25).

Considered secondary to marketing, as shown by the different emphases in his book, is what Jarvis called his "greatest hope," the use of the Internet for civic responsibility, though he refers more to censorship in China and other countries without mentioning any civic issues here in the United States (26). "Out of all the new societal norms the Internet fosters, [the] greatest hope is that future generations will enforce a doctrine of free speech with governments and institutions" (26). To enforce that doctrine of free speech, Google users anywhere must be cognizant of, and attempt to, circumvent the capitalist pillars of Google: gatekeeping and customization.

Internet portals, such as Google News, are gatekeepers. Traditionally, the purpose of gatekeeping in news media was to present the most important or most interesting news items. The motivation behind this practice was the efficient use of newsprint space or television screen time. "Gatekeeping in [the] network context involves not only selection of information but also addition, channeling, manipulation, localization, integration, disregard and deletion of information" (27). Online gatekeeping, like its print and television media counterparts, is used as a means to organize and prioritize information. This treatment of information creates biases in online media, no differently than in the print media. Indeed, the online media giants Time Warner, Disney, Bertelsmann, Viacom, and News Corporation are none other than the same five major media conglomerates offline, and recent trends have shown online news portals' reliance on mainstream media sources to be increasing (28). Fewer media sources are getting by the portal gates. Additionally, online news portals add their own biases to biases already present in the original sources. This bias is actually defined by scholars as "Googlearchy" (29). Users must be aware of "Googlearchy" and recognize that the portal construct is not immune from gatekeeping.

In addition to gatekeeping, Google's PageRank algorithim was designed to create normalized content, the first page search results. The algorithim relies on tracking the number of links a site has, for it is this number that determines the site's ranking and, hence, visibility to users. What is popular and frequently linked to is found in Internet searches, a scenario which leads to normalization as results are filtered down to the first page. Because 75% of users begin their search for online information with a search engine and seldom look beyond the first page of search results (30), a majority of people are receiving a narrow, normalized band of mass popular appeal, a dynamic not necessarily conducive to reviving enlightened public discourse. Compounding normalization is the fact that well established names, such as the top five media conglomerates, come to the Internet equipped with the pre-requisite of being found in a search: lots of links. The individual media producer does not have this advantage and so is exiled to Google oblivion: the second, or even later, search result page. Viral items are exceptions. Google's moral of universal empowerment, then, which lends credence to the Internet's potential resuscitation of civic responsibility, is contradicted by its own search algorithim.

Gatekeeping could be considered an innocuous practicality of which we should be cognizant. Normalization could be considered unfortunate, but not malicious, prioritizing. Customization is not at all innocuous. Customization is about Google gaining information. With every search and every use of Google services, Google retains information about the user. As Google 'learns' more about a user, it returns search results that closely align with the user's past choices, presents news that agrees with the user's world view, suggests movies or music the user will like, and advertises products in which the user will be interested. In this way, Google constructs the user's customized virtual space, a space I like to refer to as "MyWorld."

Incidentally, it has been shown that users believe sites employing customized news or advertisements to be of higher quality and relevance (31). Google then sells that user data to marketing and public relations entities. It is this last item which reveals Google's capitalist spirit. Google has been likened to an "ultimate economic surveillance machine and ultimate user exploitation machine" (32), and the end result of its data trawling process, in addition to niche marketing, is the creation of a MyWorld for each user in exchange for the user's virtual being.

The exchange reeks of exploitation. Netizens are boxed in, packaged, wrapped and bow-tied as data entities to be sold to the highest bidding marketers. Meanwhile, users are left to mentally languish in cozy, niche MyWorlds, absent of any provocative thought, as MyWorld is a personal cyberspace of zero dissonance, a comfort space that "creates the impression that our own narrow self-interest is all that exists." (33) MyWorld clearly has a psychological appeal to most users (34), rooted in the absence of dissonance (35).

MyWorld is merely an extrapolation of a politician's circle of "yes-men". Now, every individual can be surrounded by his own circle of "yes-men". These circles, alas, are flat and offer no dissent, no "dialogue, debate and conflict," wholly contrary to the idea of a public (36). The very homogeneity of the circles lacks the depth of differences to become three dimensional. While a public cannot be so big that a cohesive critical mass never coalesces from its deliberations, neither can it be so small, so niche, so minuscule and homogenous that becoming a public sphere is not even geometrically possible, since authentic conversation has been excised. The societal fragmentation and proliferation of public circles within the Internet populace does not nurture a reasoning public (37). The Internet's societal amputation, then, is more abstract; it is the metaphorical third dimension, the dimension which allows for a public sphere at all. In real terms, the amputation is authentic conversation: dialogue, debate and conflict. The amputation is the rational mind's voice.

Somewhere between a public too large and one too small is one that is just right, the village. In addition to rallying behind marketing and PR, Internet proponents may also unite behind the notion of the electronic global village (38). Long before the Internet became a household word, Marshall McLuhan predicted the possibility of technology bringing a global village to the world's people (39).

A mathematical approach by Marshall Van Alstyne and Eric Brynjolfsson investigates the nature of a society hooked into the electronic nervous system that McLuhan predicted, the

Internet. The analysis points to a spectrum of societal outcomes, and acknowledging that McLuhan was not entirely wrong, states a global village is only one possible outcome at one end of the spectrum. Balkanization, those myriad public circles, is at the opposite end of the spectrum (40). The possible outcomes vary depending on the nature of information infrastructure and on societal choices made regarding tolerance to dissonance. If the infrastructure favors capitalism and tolerance to new or different ideas is low, Google MyWorlds and niche marketing thrive. Given an infrastructure free of gatekeeping and customization and high dissonance tolerance among users, MyWorlds deteriorate (40). Van Alstyne's and Brynjolfsson's argument is simple: "If information technology provides a lubricant that allows for the satisfaction of preferences against the friction of geography…local heterogeneity can give way to virtual homogeneity as communities coalesce across geographic boundaries" (41).

Balkanization will occur whenever the focus on preferred interactions exceeds that of existing interactions (42). The limit on human capacity for calculation, bounded rationality, supports this statement. The human brain can only absorb so much data, can only meaningfully interact with so many people and can only do so much. This mandates that as preferred interactions increase, existing interactions will decrease, as the total number of interactions is finite and bounded by human capacity. As preferred interactions increase, the degree of balkanization increases. If, however, users seek information and interactions outside their milieu, balkanization can be reversed; that is, with a user's taste for diversity and tolerance of dissonance, integration may be fostered. Again, user preference helps dictate the societal outcome.

The potential economic cost associated with balkanization is essentially that of over-specialization. When, for example, scientists collaborate within their own field, it is often very productive. This arrangement furthers the knowledge in that field. However, the significant advantage of collaboration between scientists of different fields is precluded. Work at the boundaries of disciplines that furthers knowledge in potentially more significant ways should not be dismissed. For example, Watson and Crick combined skills from zoology and x-ray diffraction to determine the structure of DNA (42). The social cost of balkanization is a loss of societal cohesiveness and the fostering of independent public circles of homogenous peoples, isolated MyWorlds. As already discussed, the proliferation of homogenous circles compromises public discourse and leads to compromised democracy. The Internet infrastructure coupled with individual preferences offers a range of societal outcomes. The choices regarding infrastructure and user preferences determine where in the spectrum society will reside. There should be no "illusions that a greater sense of community will inexorably result" (42).

With Google firmly established, only society's choices remain to tip the scale towards either global village or balkanization. Alas, it is our social values that are imbedded in the technology (43). Given Google's algorithim of link emphasis, web-site providers capitulated, and to ensure their success under Google mandates, initiated search engine optimization (SEO), thus stabilizing Google's position. Users' ignorance of the data mining that Google employs further stabilizes Google's algorithim, as Google acquires ever more data to sell. Users also knowingly agree to the service-for-profile model and neglect to take the steps necessary to maintain, at least some, privacy. Google default settings are guaranteed to assist data collection. Meanwhile, Google continues to make recursive improvements to its algorithim based on users' actions in the ongoing social construction of technology (44).

To date, the societal tendency appears to be towards balkanization. The only major social movement initiated through the Internet, the Occupy Movement, has faded and been forgotten in short order, left to limp along online already past its prime. While there are many factors that derailed the movement, balkanization is one, sadly ironic, since it was a momentary lapse of societal integration which brought the movement together. Simply stated, the movement's cohesiveness was not sustained. The theme of class inequality central to the Occupy Movement played prominently in President Obama's 2012 State of the Union Address, but the tarnished Occupy Movement was not credited for influencing the political discussion. (45) On the other hand, at least the theme was present.

The politics of privatization also plays a role in buttressing a less democratic Internet. Government has no control over search technology or the related issues of consumer privacy, and perhaps this is a convenient arrangement for government and business: business continues its status quo of unbridled data collection, while the government relies on the use of that data when it so decides it is necessary for, say, "terrorism" concerns. The financial blockade of Wikileaks points to government and business collusion.

> In December 2010, the major payment systems used to buy goods and services online decided that Wikileaks was no longer an acceptable customer. Mastercard, Visa, and PayPal summarily cut off service, putting Wikileaks into deep financial

> trouble and further marginalizing an organization that had become an object of fear and loathing to the United States government and other centers of wealth and power. (46)

In 2011, the House of Representatives deliberated on the economic viability of ensuring network neutrality (47). Network neutrality, the idea that telecommunications carriers should not favor any content over another, has emerged as a consequence of telecommunications carriers' business collusion and conflict of interest practices. These businesses continue to fight against the Federal Communication Commission's efforts towards network neutrality, and the Whitehouse may well assist them in this fight (47). Telecommunications carriers are not alone in their attempts to gain capitalist leverage in the Internet medium. Hollywood has pressured the government to consider copyright laws, such as the Stop Online Piracy Act (SOPA), that would have resulted in Internet censorship (48). All of these business practices, alongside government or not, are evidence of capitalist birds roosting on the Internet wires, and none of these practices promotes a decentralized, democratic medium.

Unlike the Internet, the television medium, by its very epistemology, promotes a representative public sphere. McLuhan recognized television's soporific effects (49), and now, it is common knowledge that television induces passive brain activity. The Internet offers a broad range of media and, so, does not have the inherent limitation of fostering only a representative public sphere. As Van Alstyne and Brynjolfsson demonstrated, many societal outcomes are possible (40). Because the nature of a society's dominant media determines the nature of that society's public discourse, when investigating the Internet's effects on public discourse, one has to assess, not only gatekeeping, normalization, customization, privatization, and balkanization, but also which media is dominant within the Internet medium. Is Internet use being optimized towards a reasoning public sphere?

The Age of Show Business created a dominant state of mind. Entertainment became the supra-ideology, and all manner of topics were presented as entertainment, a yet ongoing television practice (50). This state of mind has colored just how the Internet medium has been adopted. Essentially, society has been stamped with the Age of Show Business mentality and seeks out, not the empowerment offered by the Internet, but the entertainment. Of the top 10 Internet activities that users engage in, obtaining news and current events was ranked 7th. The remaining 9 of 10 were related to connectivity, games, music, videos and purchasing (51). Mark

Bauerlein echoes these findings, and while Steven Johnson and Jason Mittel promote gaming and the new "sophisticated" television programming as educational, Bauerlein buries those contentions with contradictory data (52-54). In this media era, entertainment has become an art form. The multitasking enabled by the Internet allows for the near simultaneous media consumption and production that results in what I call "entertainment styling." Entertainment styling is on demand personalized entertainment in multimedia fashion. Susan Sontag writes, "…the ascendancy of a culture whose most intelligible, persuasive values are drawn from the entertainment industries has undermin[ed the] standards of seriousness" (55). Prunesquallor adds:

> The very fact of an individual being rational and informed is a monumental cultural achievement, considering that our nature tends the other way. Even the most Spock-like among us are in constant struggle with their baser desires. Becoming informed requires discipline. One has to acquire the habit of sitting still for long periods and digesting ideas and facts. It is much easier to click "*Maxim's Hottest Babes of 2011*" or "*So and So's Sordid Sex-Life Revealed* (56).

The Internet actually allows for increased avoidance of mental challenge, as more hedonistic options are just a click away. Accustomed to pleasurable pursuits and intellectual atrophy, society has embraced the Internet for its entertainment potential.

Important to note, here, is that balkanization does not necessarily imply the exclusive consumption of entertainment media, only the exclusive consumption of a narrow range of information which isolates and buffers against dissonance. Balkanization implies the disappearance of inter-group interaction. Entertainment styling, on the other hand, refers to entertainment dominance in media selection. While balkanization groups may, or may not, seek out serious topics, balkanized groups are homogenous and have no interaction between groups. Entertainment dominant groups may, or may not, be balkanized, but their interaction is of little import to civic responsibility.

When the Internet is accessed through an institution of capitalism, it succumbs to capitalist concerns and serves marketing and public relations foremost. Gatekeeping, normalization, customization, and privatization whittle away the Internet's democratic ideals forcing a shift towards a representative public sphere. The responsibility to optimize the Internet medium falls to society, and society, instead, chooses entertainment styling and balkanization.

The capitalist, privatized construct which allows Google to sell users' data to marketers causes the Internet as a whole to become an enormous marketing boondoggle. Further, society's choice to accept the 'free' island states of MyWorld burdens society with costs it cannot afford: less interdisciplinary collaboration and the loss of authentic conversation in the public sphere. The Internet, through our own social constructions of its design, through capitalist influence, and through the ignorant, apathetic or indifferent entertainment mindset, is merely the *schein* of what it could be, instead of the *sein* of a new age of enlightenment and democratic empowerment. Society remains stagnant in a representative public sphere at the vapid end of the societal spectrum and remains there by its very choices and values. However, this does not have to be so. The Internet, unlike television, offers a range of societal outcomes, from representative to reasoning publics. Despite the established capitalist forces acting on the Internet, society has yet the power to dictate at any time where it will reside in that spectrum.

References

1. M. McLuhan, *Understanding Media: The Extensions of Man* (New York: McGraw Hill, 1964) pp. 11
2. N. Postman, *Amusing Ourselves to Death: Public Discourse in the Age of Show Business* (United States: Viking Penguin Inc., 1985) pp. 161 - 163
3. N. Postman, *Amusing Ourselves to Death: Public Discourse in the Age of Show Business* (United States: Viking Penguin Inc., 1985) pp. 83
4. H. Trenz, "Digital Media and the Return of the Representative Public Sphere," *Javnost — The Public* **16.1**, 33 – 46 (2009), EBSCO.,Web. 18 July 2012, pp. 35
5. H. Trenz, "Digital Media and the Return of the Representative Public Sphere," *Javnost — The Public* **16.1**, 33 – 46 (2009), EBSCO, Web, 18 July 2012, pp. 34
6. Bauerlein, Mark, *The Dumbest Generation: How the Digital Age Stupefies Young Americans and Jeopardizes Our Future or Don't Trust Anyone Under 30* (New York: Penguin Books, 2008) Print, pp. 212 (Jefferson qtd. in Bauerlein)
7. H. Trenz, "Digital Media and the Return of the Representative Public Sphere," *Javnost — The Public* **16.1**, 33 – 46 (2009), EBSCO, Web, 18 July 2012, pp. 36
8. H. Trenz, "Digital Media and the Return of the Representative Public Sphere," *Javnost — The Public* **16.1**, 33 – 46 (2009), EBSCO, Web, 18 July 2012, pp. 34-37
9. M. McLuhan, and Q. Fiore with J. Agel, *The Medium is the Massage: An Inventory of Effects* (New York: Random House, 1967) pp. 8
10. N. Postman, *Amusing Ourselves to Death: Public Discourse in the Age of Show Business* (United States: Viking Penguin Inc., 1985) pp. 155 - 163
11. "NDAA on trial: White House refuses to abide with ban against indefinite detention of Americans," RT.com, TV Novosti, 10 Aug. 2012, Web, 11 Aug. 2012
    http://rt.com/usa/news/ndaa-injunction-tangerine-detention-376/
12. E. Bucy, and M. Grabe, "Taking Television Seriously: A Sound and Image Bite Analysis of Presidential Campaign Coverage," *Journal of Communication* **57**, 652 – 675 (2007), Communication & Mass Media Complete, Web, 15 July 2012

13. P. Moy, M. Xenos, and V. Hess, "Communication and Citizenship: Mapping the Political Effects of Infotainment," *Mass Communication & Society* **8.2** 111- 131 (2005), Communication & Mass Media Complete, Web, 15 July 2012

14. N. Postman, *Amusing Ourselves to Death: Public Discourse in the Age of Show Business* (United States: Viking Penguin Inc., 1985) pp. 16

15. E. Bucy, and M. Grabe, "Taking Television Seriously: A Sound and Image Bite Analysis of Presidential Campaign Coverage," *Journal of Communication* **57** 655 (2007), Communication & Mass Media Complete, Web, 15 July 2012 (Drew & Grimes, 1987; Grimes, 1991; Lang, 1995 qtd. in Bucy & Grabe 655)

16. N. Postman, *Amusing Ourselves to Death: Public Discourse in the Age of Show Business* (United States: Viking Penguin Inc., 1985) pp. 142-154

17. M. Bauerlein, *The Dumbest Generation: How the Digital Age Stupefies Young Americans and Jeopardizes Our Future or Don't Trust Anyone Under 30* (New York: Penguin Books, 2008) pp. 212

18. T. Leary, *Flashbacks A Personal and Cultural History of an Era* (Los Angeles: Jeremy P. Tarcher, Inc., 1983) pp. 253

19. A. Mager, "Algorithmic Ideology," *Information, Communication & Society* **15.5** 771 (2012)

20. J. Jarvis, *What Would Google Do?* (New York: Harper Collins, 2009) pp. 11-23, 48-53

21. C. Self, "Hegel, Habermas, and Community: The Public in the New Media Era," *International Journal of Strategic Communication* **4.2** 78 – 92 (2010), Communication & Mass Media Complete, Web, 14 July 2012, pp. 78-90

22. A. Ries, & L. Ries, *The Fall of Advertising and the Rise of PR* (New York: Harper Collins, 2004) pp. 247

23. T. Cooley, "Interactive Communication — Public Relations on the Web," *Public Relations Quarterly* **44.2** 41 – 42 (1999), Communication & Mass Media Complete, Web, 14 July 2012, pp. 42

24. T. Cooley, "Interactive Communication — Public Relations on the Web," *Public Relations Quarterly* **44.2** 41 – 42 (1999), Communication & Mass Media Complete, Web, 14 July 2012, pp. 41-42

25. J. Jarvis, *What Would Google Do?* (New York: Harper Collins, 2009) pp. 67

26. J. Jarvis, *What Would Google Do?* (New York: Harper Collins, 2009) pp. 237

27. C. Bui, "Examining the New Gatekeepers: News Portal's Inclusion and Ranking of Media and Events," Conference Papers — International Communication Association 2009 *Communication & Mass Media Complete*, Web, 15 July 2012, pp. 4

28. C. Bui, "Examining the New Gatekeepers: News Portal's Inclusion and Ranking of Media and Events," Conference Papers — International Communication Association 2009 *Communication & Mass Media Complete*, Web, 15 July 2012, pp. 19

29. C. Bui, "Examining the New Gatekeepers: News Portal's Inclusion and Ranking of Media and Events," Conference Papers — International Communication Association 2009 *Communication & Mass Media Complete*, Web, 15 July 2012, pp. 6

30. C. Bui, "Examining the New Gatekeepers: News Portal's Inclusion and Ranking of Media and Events," Conference Papers — International Communication Association 2009 *Communication & Mass Media Complete*, Web, 15 July 2012, pp. 2

31. J. Beier, and S. Kalyanaram, "The Psychological Appeal of MyNews.com; The Interplay Between Customization and Recommendation Sources in News Websites," Conference Papers — International Communication Association 2008: 1- 37, Communication & Mass Media Complete, Web, 15 July 2012, pp. 27

32. A. Mager, "Algorithmic Ideology," *Information, Communication & Society* **15.5** 772 (2012) (Fuchs 2011 qtd. in Mager)

33. J. Gardner, "When Machines Decide What We 'Think'," *Nieman Reports* **65.2** 20 (2011) (Pariser qtd in Gardner)

34. J. Beier, and S. Kalyanaram, "The Psychological Appeal of MyNews.com; The Interplay Between Customization and Recommendation Sources in News Websites," Conference Papers — International Communication Association 2008: 1- 37, Communication & Mass Media Complete, Web, 15 July 2012, pp. 1-32

35. S. Baran, *Introduction to Mass Media/Media Literacy and Culture* (New York: McGrawHill, 2010) pp. 365

36. C. Self, "Hegel, Habermas, and Community: The Public in the New Media Era," *International Journal of Strategic Communication* **4.2** 78 – 92 (2010) Communication & Mass Media Complete, Web, 14 July 2012, pp. 78-90

37. H. Trenz, "Digital Media and the Return of the Representative Public Sphere," *Javnost — The Public* **16.1** 33 – 46 (2009), EBSCO, Web, 18 July 2012, pp. 44

38. L. Grossman, "Time's Person of the Year: You," *Time* **168.26** 38-41 (2006)

39. M. McLuhan, *Understanding Media: The Extensions of Man*, (New York: McGraw Hill, 1964) pp. 3

40. M. Van Alstyne & E. Brynjolfsson, "Electronic Communities: Global Village or Cyberbalkans?", 17th International Conference on Information Systems, Cleveland, OH, Dec. 1996, Address, pp. 3

41. M. Van Alstyne & E. Brynjolfsson, "Electronic Communities: Global Village or Cyberbalkans?", 17th International Conference on Information Systems, Cleveland, OH, Dec. 1996, Address, pp. 3-4

42. M. Van Alstyne & E. Brynjolfsson, "Electronic Communities: Global Village or Cyberbalkans?", 17th International Conference on Information Systems, Cleveland, OH, Dec. 1996, Address, pp. 22

43. A. Mager, "Algorithmic Ideology," *Information, Communication & Society* **15.5** 773 (2012)

44. A. Mager, "Algorithmic Ideology," *Information, Communication & Society* **15.5** 769-784 (2012)

45. Obama, Barack President, "State of the Union Address 2012," NBC. KOBI, Medford, 24 Jan. 2012, Television

46. D. Gillmor, "Meanwhile in the Land of the Free…" *Columbia Journalism Review* **51.1** 28–30 (2012), Communication & Mass Media Complete, Web, 14 July 2012, pp. 28

47. United States, Committee on Energy and Commerce, House of Representatives, *Network Neutrality and Internet Regulation: Warranted or More Economic Harm Than Good?*, Washington, GPO, 2011

48. D. Gillmor, "Meanwhile in the Land of the Free…" *Columbia Journalism Review* **51.1** 28–30 (2012), Communication & Mass Media Complete, Web, 14 July 2012, pp. 29

49. M. McLuhan, *Understanding Media: The Extensions of Man* (New York: McGraw Hill, 1964)

50. N. Postman, *Amusing Ourselves to Death: Public Discourse in the Age of Show Business* (United States: Viking Penguin Inc., 1985) pp. 87

51. S. Baran, *Introduction to Mass Media/Media Literacy and Culture* (New York: McGrawHill, 2010) pp. 271

52. M. Bauerlein, *The Dumbest Generation: How the Digital Age Stupefies Young Americans and Jeopardizes Our Future or Don't Trust Anyone Under 30* (New York: Penguin Books, 2008) pp. 71-161

53. S. Johnson, *Everything Bad is Good for You* (New York: Penguin Group, 2005) pp. 15-201

54. J. Mittel, *Television and American Culture* (United States: Oxford University Press, 2009)

55. "Dumbing Down," *Kazumitna*, Word Press, Web, 10 July 2012, (Sontag qtd in Kazumitna.com)
http://kazumitna.com/antimuzak/?page_id=154

56. ""Vikileaks," The New Media, and the Debasement of the Public Discourse," Dr. Prunesquallor, Word Press, 02 February 2012, Web. 10 July 2012,
http://drprunesquallor.wordpress.com/tag/vikileaks/

A Closer Look at the Early Detection and Prevention of School Shootings

Shelley-Ann Hincks – Southern Oregon University

Abstract

In response to the latest school shooting at Sandy Hook Elementary School, in which 20 children and six adults lost their lives, President Obama talked about a new gun law and attempted to place a ban on assault rifles *(14)*. News stations reported on sheriff's departments around the nation reacting to this by saying that they would not implement this law, should it get passed. In a report on gun laws in the US, Wals , concludes that, "America has the highest gun homicide rate of all developed countries", and that "Americans own 35 percent to 50 percent of the world's civilian guns" *(10)* Wals, also states that, "America's gun laws are the most lax in the developed world with no federal regulations banning the semiautomatic assault weapons or large-capacity ammo magazines often used in mass shootings" *(10)*. This paper examines what the school system can do to protect itself from the lethal combination of an angry young person armed with deadly weapons and proposes a critical look at the access that children have to weapons in their homes.

    The American Department of Education needs to empower itself with solid and applicable solutions designed with the main focus of preventing school shootings. Teachers and administration staff are trained to handle school violence: a comprehensive meta-analysis of anger management and other impulse control programs *(4)*, implemented in schools across America confirms that something is being done toward the handling of inappropriate behavior in schools. The issue is that although there are systems available to deal with mental instability or excessive and aggressive behavior in schools, a fresh and substantial analysis is needed as to whether these systems and programs are effective in the early detection and subsequent prevention of school shootings.

    As stated by Candelaria, et. al *(4)*, a number of systems and programs are at present being implemented and utilized by many of the schools in America, but most are geared toward at-risk students and their efforts focus on the prevention of violent behavior. A feasible concept when considering that a school's primary responsibility for the management of student behavior is from the point that the student is on the school's premises or on their way to and from school. Effectively placing the school and its staff in the position of dealing with "whoever walks through the door" *(4)*.

    All schools have school safety policies, and codes of conduct. Reece, suggests that many of these codes of conduct are antique documents. This means that "some have never been clearly conceptualized, because although "new *problem behaviors*" have emerged in students, like "*hooded jackets and cell phones*", these have simply been added to a laundry list of banned behaviors" *(9)*. Reece further suggests that, "a fresh look at school disciplines regarding suspension and expulsion would bring this section of school management into the modern day era, and that school discipline systems should be overhauled [because] in the past, suspension was most likely an effective solution, but, today alternative methods might have a greater impact on changing inappropriate student behavior, saying that traditional actions have focused on *"exclusionary"* consequences for wayward students such as suspension and expulsion" *(9)*.

When evaluating what school principals, teachers and administration staff may need in regard to protecting schools from violence, the law should take into consideration how the staffs of a school are going to be able to define a potential shooter out of the numerous children they manage daily. It is certainly fair to expect them to monitor aggressive behavior, even the violent acts of one child upon another. It may be asking too much, however, to expect them to have the skills or qualifications to detect or predict by means of studying behavior what a student might do in the future. A cautionary look is suggested toward complimentary systems that could network or interlace with systems existing. Systems, which at present are not, nor will be in the immediate future, adequately prepared for this particular kind of violence.

In order to build on the existing systems, a more refined look at them might be appropriate before making any decisions for change or enhancement. Presently, school staff functions under license of the mandatory training on how to cope with victims of bullying and other incidents that can happen in a school day. The public should consider whether the answer is to allow schools to become barricaded secure facilities by integrating iris and face recognition devices, and having armed guards at entrance doors or worse, armed teachers.

It is necessary here to mention that bullying in schools has long been associated with school shootings, and is widely believed to be the precursor to many of these events. In an evaluation of State Bullying Laws and Policies by Stuart-Cassel, a document that was presented to the US Department of Education in 2011, states that "The Columbine High School shooting in 1999, was the first of many incidents that seemed to implicate bullying as an underlying cause to school shootings". Declaring that, "bullying is being viewed as a urgent, social, health and education concern," and that "officials and members of the school systems are presently looking at bullying as a very serious issue" (as referenced in Green & Ross, 2005, p. ix). Stuart-Cassel continued by reporting that bullying is under-managed by society - not studied to the depth that it should be - and all too often leads to real trauma for the victims *(12)*. Bullying destroys the popular assumption that school is a safe and positive learning environment, and rather creates an environment of fear that can very quickly reach uncontrollable levels.

Facts that support these issues of bullying in school environments come from a paper written by Marisa, Vossekuil, Fein, & Modzeleski and are posted by the US Department of Justice/Office of Justice Programs: Fast Facts about Bullying are *(11)*:

1. In an OJJDP survey, 13.2 percent of participants reported having been physically bullied during the previous year.
2. In the US, 13 percent of 6th-through 10th grade student's bully, and 6 percent are both victims and bullies.
3. In a survey of American middle and high school students, 66 percent of bullying victims believed school professionals responded poorly to bullying problems.
4. Bullying takes place more often at school than on the way to and from school. Bullying is highlighted here as most shooters have been bullied at school in some form.

A review of the above noted points 3 and 4 allows us the opportunity to see a pattern evolve. First the child is bullied, and then school professionals handle the incident poorly. This may be the first area of existing protocols that can be uplifted in the form of refresher training courses geared toward the management of bullying in schools.

At present, it would seem that schools have no remedy for the particular mix of violence involved in a school shooting. There is no possible way for schools and their staff to protect themselves from something that they have no control over: they are unable to secure weapons in these children's homes. They are also unable to control the home environment and how the children are influenced to deal with problems in their lives. Given the facts in an article written by Kaylen, on the association of youth violence and social disorganization (p.1), and another by Jaffe, Karriker, Foshee, & Ennett, which discusses, "understanding how neighborhoods influence the development of youth violence" *(7)*. These two papers support the concept that schools essentially come in at the tail end of the problems that start at home. Therefore leaving schools to defend themselves against enraged teenagers that have easy access to deadly weapons who then decide to walk through the door.

Research addressing school shootings and threats of school shootings by adolescents has emerged out of necessity to address the issue. According to Booth, "there is evidence that many school shooters in past cases have displayed odd or aggressive behavior, long before the actual event took place," such as, "many of them publicly announcing their threats in the form of verbal communication and email[s] to their friends"*(1)*. Booth also mentions that, "obvious warning signals were prevalent", which then begs the question of why something was not done to prevent them, *(1)*.

In hindsight, these "apparently obvious warning signals" *(1)* still does not enable anyone to compile a profile of how a potential shooter will behave. These crimes are complex in nature and intertwined with many other factors such a socio-economic environment, social bonds, family dynamics, peer relationships and opinion of self. Ching offers "a new phenomenon called appetitive violence, related to youth committing violence for thrill seeking" *(5)*. Also, in a study by National Center for the Analysis of Violent Crime (NCAVC, 1999), an important fact was highlighted: that fact being the encouragement of students to come forward with information about "*Leakage*" - a term O'Toole uses for, "when a student intentionally or unintentionally reveals clues of feelings, thoughts, fantasies, attitudes, or intentions that may signal an impending violent act" *(8)*. This confirms that this is a multi-faceted problem with many different areas that deserve more study. This author believes that a bird's eye view of how shooters have behaved in the past will go a long way to inform and educate on behavioral signals that could be interpreted early, and used in the prevention of violence of this nature.

A few of these behaviors are studied by O'Tool and reported in the document (NCAVC threat assessment-intervention model report), suggesting that the "one response to the pressure for action may be an effort to identify the next shooter by developing a "profile" of the typical shooter", which "may sound like a reasonable preventative measure" but reasons that "trying to draw up a catalogue or *checklist* of warning signs to detect a potential school shooter can be shortsighted, and even dangerous" *(8)*. Proposing rather that a "Four Pronged Assessment Model" be utilized, based on the "totality of the circumstances", known about the student in four major areas such as: the personality of the student, the family and school dynamics, the student's role in these, and lastly the student's social dynamics *(8)*.

The complexity of these crimes features many different arenas that require further study into the psychology of school shooters. The subject that will be addressed and needs to be highlighted is the access that these children have to some of the most lethal weapons in the world; the argument being that without the weapons these crimes cannot take place.

A paper by Burke, about juvenile culpability and brain formation of youth, which discusses the development of brain function and teenage cognitive capabilities, and citing Feld, notes that "Teenagers make poorer decisions than adults because of basic psychological, neurobiological, physical, and developmental differences" *(1)*. Burke also takes a closer look at, "the reasons youth are not allowed to assume adult responsibilities, such as entering into contracts, purchasing alcohol, getting married without a parent's consent, and voting is because of their poor decision making" *(1)*. An addition can be made to this list: purchasing a gun, as teenagers are not legally allowed to purchase guns for the very same reasons. This thought should begin serious consideration regarding the dangers of teenagers having easy access to guns in their homes. Vossekuil, Reddy, Borum, & Modzeleski in a paper on "The Final Report and findings of the Safe School Initiative", offers some insight into some of the facts about a few of the shootings that have taken place at schools in recent years *(13)*: The shooters had access to guns, (either from their own home or that of a relative). Most shooters did behave in a manner that had caused concern indicating a child in trouble, some even to the point of being expelled from the schools that they attacked. Shooters have told at least one person if not many, of their intentions. All of the attacks are planned in advance with specific targets in mind, and are not impulsive.

The suggestions of solutions mentioned so far are applicable; having said that, they only highlight the argument. Although they could play a very important role in managing violence in schools, they may not or cannot offer the system a way to stop children from gaining access to lethal weapons. It is not the Education Department's (ED) place to usurp the 2nd Amendment (The Right to Bear Arms). The true answer might be to look at what safety measures are exercised in the homes of teens that have access to these weapons. The ED needs to first establish the right to the intimate knowledge of a troubled student if the need arises to warrant. It then needs to take heed of the words of President Obama, quoted in a Press Release (2013) by Secretary Duncan, US Secretary of Education, "We can limit access to the deadliest guns and ammunition, and we can put in checks to keep guns out of the wrong hands. We can also provide new resources, so schools can develop and implement comprehensive emergency management plans"(14*)*. These words are words of hope and an indication that the world is taking notice.

In conclusion, and in offering a solid and applicable solution toward the prevention of even one more school shooting, a more intense analysis of behavior displayed by school shooters in the past, and prior to the shooting incident is needed. Moreover, a critical evaluation of what the education system is presently lacking in resources of how to identify what sort of weapons teens have access to in their homes, or relative's homes. A notable assessment of how parents can be more accountable for the weapons kept in their houses. Some parents may not agree with this, but need to discern between the loss of privacy against the cost, which is the life of a child and often times many children. Harsher penalties could be legislated and put into place regarding the security of weapons kept in the home. Awareness campaigns can inform parents of the severe consequences that may be faced in the event of one of their children being associated with any incident involving a weapon on school grounds.

References

1. B. Booth, Ph.D., V. B. Van Hasselt, Ph.D., G. M. Vecchi, Ph.D., Addressing school violence. *U.S. Secret Service.* (2002)

2. A. S. Burke, Department of criminology and criminal justice, Southern Oregon University. Under Construction: Brian Formation, culpability, and the criminal justice system. Elsevier Ltd. International. *Journal of Law and Psychiatry.* **34,** 381-385.

3. B. Vossekuil *et al.*, An interim report on the prevention of targeted violence in school. *Washington, DC; U.S. Secret Service, National Threat Assessment Center* (2000).

4. A. Candelaria, A. Fedewa, S. Ahn, The effects of anger management on children's social and emotional outcomes: A meta-analysis. *School Psychology International.* **33.6***, 596-614 (2012).* DOI: 10.117/0143034312454360.

5. H. Ching, M. Daffern, S. Thomas, Appetitive violence: A new phenomenon? *Psychiatry, Psychology & Law.* **(19)5***, 745-763 (November 2011).* DOI:10.1080/13218719.2011.623338

6. K. J. Karriker-Jaffe, Ph.D., V. A. Foshee, Ph.D., S. T. Ennett, Ph.D., Examining how neighborhood disadvantage influences trajectories of adolescent violence: A look at social bonding and psychological distress. *Journal of School Health.* **81(12),** 764-773 (November 2011). DOI: 10.1111/j.1746-1561.2011.00656.x

7. M. T. Kaylen, W. A. Pridemore, A reassessment of the association between social disorganization and youth violence in rural Areas. *Social Science Quarterly.* **92(4)**, 978-1001. (October 2011). DOI: 10.1111/j.1540-6237.2011.00808.x

8. M. E. O'Tool, Ph.D., The school shooter: a threat assessment perspective. (*FBI Academy, Quantico, Va. 1999;* http://www.fbi.gov/stats-services/publications/school-shooter)

9. L. P. Reece, Ph.D., What every administrator needs to know about alternatives suspension and expulsion. (*Univ. of Nebraska* http://www.mslbd.org/Admin_Conference/Peterson%2010-6-06.pdf)

10. B. Wals, Arms race time. *Vocational and Career Collections.* **181(1)**, 14-15. (February 2013).

11. R. Marisa *et al.*, Evaluating risk for targeted violence in schools: comparing risk assessment, threat assessment, and other approaches. *Psychology in the Schools*, **38(2)**, (February 2001). DOI: 10.1002/pits.1007

12. V. Stuart-Cassel, A. Bell, J. F. Springer, Analysis of state bullying laws and policies. *(Dept. of Education* http://www2.ed.gov/rschstat/eval/bullying/state-bullying-laws/state-bullying-laws.pdf)

13. B. Vossekuil *et al.*, The final report of the safe school initiative. *U.S. Secret Service and U.S. Dept. of Educ.* (1990).

14. Secretary Duncan (US Secretary of Education) in a statement on the President's recommendations on reducing gun violence in schools. *Senate Appropriations Subcommittee on Labor, Health and Human Services, Education, and Other Related Agencies Press Release*, (April 2013; http://www.ed.gov/news/speeches/statement-us-secretary-education-arne-duncanfy-2014-budget-request)

Eye Am Watching You: CCTV - The Metal Ring of Hope

A Study of the Use of Closed Circuit Television

Jason Getty - Southern Oregon University

Abstract

Close circuit television (CCTV) cameras are not only being used in abundance in the United Kingdom, but on a global scale in the criminal justice community. The main reason for CCTV camera usage is for the prevention and reduction of crime, yet several different studies that will be discussed in this paper have shown that CCTV cameras are not an effective tool in reducing, preventing or deterring crime. This study looks at different public perceptions of CCTV and howl it invades into their private lives and looks at CCTV camera use from a political point-of-view. This study will also examine results from a survey that was conducted to determine the opinions of students attending Southern Oregon University which included a mixture of gender, age, ethnicity and educational degree majors.

"They that can give up essential liberty to obtain a little temporary safety deserve neither liberty nor safety." - Benjamin Franklin

Close circuit television (CCTV) use has grown significantly within the recent years, in various nations around the world. Surveillance cameras in England and Wales increased from "100 in 1990 to 400 in 1994, 5,200 in 1997 and 40,000 in 2002" (*1*). "It is estimated that there are approximately 4.2 million cameras monitoring the public in the United Kingdom, equating to one camera for every 14 people" (*1*). CCTV is a hot topic within the criminal justice system. Some see CCTV as a useful tool in order to reduce and prevent crime. Some see it as an attack on civil liberties while others see it as a proper response in order to effectively deter, prevent and reduce crime and disorder within a complex, highly populated community.

Cohen and Felson's Routine Activities Theory states, "[i]n order for crime to occur three necessary elements must converge in time and space: a motivated offender, suitable target and lack of a capable guardian" (*2*). Having a capable guardian can interrupt the motivated offender from interacting with the suitable target. CCTV cameras are being used worldwide to not only combat crime, but to combat anti-social behavior to ensure that public morals are monitored and public order is secured. After all, CCTV cameras are 24-hour a day capable guardians, they never need to eat, sleep, smoke or take a bathroom break. Billions of dollars are spent on CCTV cameras each year worldwide in the belief that their use is the be-all, end-all solution to prevent crime. There is little evidence to show that crime is even being reduced because of CCTV. This does not mean that CCTV cannot be successful in reducing and deterring crime, but it does not work in all situations. Many studies have found mixed results with the deployment of CCTV cameras. Even with mixed results, the general public seems to approve of CCTV camera use in order to prevent and reduce crime.

Literature Review

Caplan, Kennedy and Petrossian (3) conducted a study to look at how crime is deterred by implementation of strategic vs. non-strategic placements of CCTV cameras (3). Caplan, Kennedy and Petrossian looked at new methods for the implementation of CCTV cameras in order to determine new ways to target crime in Newark, NJ, and then analyzed the effectiveness of CCTV in deterring and reducing crime (3).

This study examined the reliability of CCTV cameras and how they impacted the validity of their study by evaluating crime areas and how CCTV cameras were used in order to study the impact of CCTV use had on crime and how effectively CCTV cameras worked. By measuring the deterrence of crime by police-monitored CCTV cameras for street crimes in Newark, NJ, and how a specific time frame and what type of cameras were strategically placed in public, their study could reasonably measure the impact CCTV cameras had on preventing, reducing and deterring criminal activity.

Dome cameras were used in their study because they have the greatest range of motion and create the perception that people are being watched from all angles. Dome cameras provide surveillance in a wider angle of view (including "gray areas") and not just the target area itself. The study found that "strategically placing cameras showed no difference [when] comparing it to non-strategic placements for trying to reduce and prevent crime" (3). Even though CCTV might not be the most effective tool in combating all crime, it is possible that it can deter some crime (not by a large percentage) by proper strategic location and implementation of CCTV cameras within a city. If the proper cameras are used (dome cameras because they have a 360 degree of view) CCTV might be an effective tool in order to combat crime. It is important to know what type of environment surrounds the camera and how far apart they are in order to achieve the maximum effect of deterring crime. Overall, further research and evaluation is required in order to determine how, where and when they are used and that CCTV cameras should be used to target specific crimes under specific conditions.

The implementation of CCTV cameras exists, not only in the United States, but are being implemented by the millions in the United Kingdom. Farrington, Gill, Waples and Argomaniz (2007) conducted a study to analyze the overall effect of CCTV on crime on a large scale in the United Kingdom. They studied multiple sites and analyzed the impact the cameras had on reducing crime (*4*).

CCTV was implemented in various areas including residential, town and city centers, one hospital and parking lots. Data was collected from before and after the CCTV cameras were installed in specified target and control locations. The study found that CCTV cameras were not effective in reducing crime in train stations, parking lots, residential or city centers. If CCTV was to be effective, it would depend on how it was implemented, how the cameras were positioned, how the operators were monitoring the control room, and require effective communication with the police in order to deter, prevent and reduce crime.

Furthermore, Norris and McCahill (*5*) conducted a study to evaluate how CCTV was being used in the United Kingdom and why was it being used to deter crime (*5*). The study examined how CCTV was being used at a macro and micro level, starting with how CCTV had become so popular within the United Kingdom. Norris and McCahill particularly looked at to what extent were CCTV cameras being used in order to prevent and deter crime (*5*). Norris and McCahill observed the functions of the control rooms where CCTV cameras were being monitored in order to evaluate four different environments: residential housing, public streets, train stations and shopping malls (*5*). Norris and McCahill found that in some instances CCTV can be used to catch criminals, but CCTV was becoming a form of penal modernism that was being used to punish the public as a whole in regards to privacy in order to prevent and deter crime (*5*). The study determined that CCTV was nothing more than the state extending their controlling power upon the masses.

Moreover, Taylor (*1*) conducted a study on CCTV cameras in order to evaluate the effectiveness of CCTV and if it contributes to crime reduction and prevention within the United Kingdom (*1*). Taylor also examined the aspect of reduction of fear among the public if more CCTV cameras were used to reduce, deter and prevent crime (*1*). Taylor examined the problem by analyzing how CCTV cameras should be evaluated, what types of crimes should CCTV cameras target, and will CCTV cameras be effective in deterring, preventing and reducing crime? (*1*). Taylor considered what types of cameras should be used and where they should positioned, how good was the field of view, and was there a good level of light so that the images were of good quality in order to determine the effectiveness of detecting and deterring crime (*1*).

CCTV camera use should consider the intentional and unintentional outcomes of their usage. The use of CCTV should consider the objectives of why CCTV is being used and will it be effective at reaching those objectives? Taylor found that the effectiveness of CCTV cameras and how they were used was inconclusive and that CCTV cameras were not effective in reducing, preventing and deterring crime (*1*). Additionally, another study exists on re-deployable CCTV (RCCTV) cameras and how non-effective they were in reducing crime within society. Re-deployable cameras are cameras that can be moved from one location to another within an environment to monitor activity.

Waples and Gill (*6*) conducted a study in the United Kingdom for a year in two different geographical locations. They stated that "this research is to understand the effectiveness of RCCTV cameras while comparing it to police recorded crime figures in order to prevent, reduce and deter crime" (*6*). Being able to measure the effectiveness of CCTV cameras is a complicated issue. Waples and Gill looked at the measurement of crime before and after the cameras were installed in a target and a control area (*6*). Waples and Gill (2006) found that "in terms of reducing crime levels and increasing the feelings of safety, RCCTV cameras were not successful in both the target and control areas" (*6*). Crime did in fact increase in both areas and it did not make the people feel safer. If RCCTV cameras are going to be effective, they must be implemented in the right areas and target specific crimes, not just crime in general. RCCTV cameras must be closely monitored to be the effective in preventing, reducing and deterring crime. There should be more than just one RCCTV camera deployed in public since it makes it difficult for the operator monitoring the cameras to track the offender from one location to the next without multiple camera locations.

Perception of CCTV Cameras

Waiton explains why are more CCTV cameras are being used in today's society (*7*). Waiton was involved in an anti-CCTV campaign in Glasgow, Scotland; particularly, why were they being used, not only in high crime areas, but in many areas that have very little criminal activity in Scotland (*7*). Waiton further asked the question of why CCTV is growing within an anti-political environment, and why are CCTV cameras and surveillance becoming so significant in today's society (*7*). Waiton used the examples above to focus on the main point of this paper by examining why CCTV cameras were being used in over abundantly in the United Kingdom (*7*). Waiton examined the problem by analyzing several arguments on why CCTV cameras were a logical solution to crime prevention and how the "elite ruling class," both of the political left and right, chooses to aggressively enforce their power over their "inferiors" through increased surveillance in society today. Furthermore, society should become more interactive with one another, without government interference, in order to curb anti-social behavior. Waiton determined that the public does not care about policing one another, and prefer to have government intervention to solve society's problems (*7*). Additionally, there has been more research conducted on CCTV cameras in Spain.

Clavell, Lojo, & Romero (*8*) examined the CCTV problem in Spain to "contribute a general empirical account of the Spanish context to the literature regarding the increase of video surveillance at a time when the boom in research on surveillance coincides with the exponential growth of CCTV cameras in Spain" (*8*). At a time when CCTV cameras seem to be popular within the criminal justice community, the research and the implementation of CCTV cameras are occurring at the same time.

Their study included analysis of various types of literature regarding CCTV cameras being deployed at a national and regional level and conducted semi-structured interviews with the people who were responsible for CCTV camera deployment in Spain. The study researched 17 different areas in Spain and the different types of regulations, rules and laws regarding CCTV camera use in those areas.

The interviews in their study were the main aspects in which to form a basis on how CCTV cameras were being used in the 17 different areas and allowed their study to compare how and why CCTV cameras were deployed in each area. The study reviewed archived data pertaining to one regional body that was responsible for CCTV camera deployment and a "media analysis through online search engines and newspaper libraries in order to follow cues obtained during interviews and the review of the archived data" (8). The study also researched CCTV camera use at an international level to provide an in depth analysis of CCTV cameras in order to understand the growth of CCTV cameras outside Western and Northern Europe.

Clavell, Lojo, & Romero found that the public perception on the use of CCTV cameras seemed to show positive results. About (68.7 percent) of the Spanish population favored the use of CCTV cameras, (66.4 percent) said that it made them feel safer, (18 percent) said it was useful in proper identification of the offenders and (15.2 percent) said that it helped prevent crime. What seems strange is that (79.4 percent) were against it in regards to loss of privacy (8). So, it seems that the people of Spain want some type of protection against crime as long as it does not intrude on their private lives.

What seems to be a contradiction in terms, if (66.4 percent) feel safer but only (15.2 percent) say it helps prevent crime, then how can a majority "feel safer" when the majority feels that it doesn't prevent crime? Are CCTV cameras creating a false sense of security?

Furthermore, the use of CCTV within society ultimately serves another purpose for policymakers, that is to say, the ultimate goal to observe, know and be in ultimate control of individuals within a society and to convince society that CCTV is the ultimate answer to effectively combat crime.

CCTV and Politics

Zurawski focused his study on why five CCTV cameras have been taken down from a small plaza in Hamburg, Germany (9). Zurawski looked into the history behind why CCTV camera use started in Hamburg in 2004 (9). Zurawski evaluated the people involved and the role they played and the lines of argumentation against the background of the political developments in Hamburg ever since the first CCTV camera was installed on the open streets of Hamburg (9). Zurawski conducted an evaluation on how CCTV cameras were becoming more than just a crime prevention tool, but being used as a political tool to spy on and an attempt to control the citizens of Hamburg as well (*9*).

In 2005, cameras were introduced in crime hot spots in Hamburg. Crime hot spots are areas where crime is high and the patterns which certain crimes happen are highly predictable. Two years later, those cameras were taken down for a particular reason. Zurawski points out that the deployment of CCTV cameras in Hamburg was politically motivated (*9*). When new people stepped into political leadership, the implementation policy and deployment of CCTV cameras were changed. Additionally, similar studies have been highlighted in Italy.

Fonio focused his study towards four key issues on CCTV use in Italy, investigating how CCTV cameras are implemented, how it changed overtime depending on who is in power, CCTV urban security policies and how they affected the general populace, and an analysis of the empirical data on the city of Milan, Italy (*10*). Fonio's findings concluded that there was a lack of data concerning the crime rate in Milan, before and after the installation of CCTV cameras (*10*). Fonio pointed out that the government claimed that it would safeguard the privacy rights of its citizens while in public, but it failed to do so (*10*). Even though the study focused on addressing how CCTV cameras were regulated, there needed to be a way to evaluate the laws and legislative framework and a need to evaluate why CCTV cameras were being implemented. The public should be the driving force to ensure that the government stays on a straight course and follows the laws and regulations regarding CCTV camera implementation and deployment.

Methodology

This current study employed a research designed 21-question survey designed to determine if participants believe that CCTV cameras are effective at reducing and deterring crime. Surveys are used quite frequently as a research method and used when "researchers are interested in experiences, attitudes, perceptions or beliefs of individuals" (*11*). The survey administered in this study was conducted with the assumption that most participants have had some type of interaction with CCTV cameras in the past.

Population

This study focused on undergraduate students at Southern Oregon University between the ages of 18-56 years old who were enrolled in introductory classes in order to determine if CCTV cameras would be effective in reducing crime.

Sample

This was a convenient sample of individuals based upon age, gender, ethnicity and educational degree major. Convenient samples are chosen because participants are easily and readily available, it is inexpensive and because the researcher does not take into account that selecting participants is representative of the entire population. Convenience samples "may or may not represent the population that is being studied therefore, generalizations about the population cannot be considered to be valid" (*11*). However, convenience sampling can be used as a starting point on which future research may be based. It is important that the researcher describes how the sample is different from that of a sample that was randomly selected. Researchers must also point out those participants who are left out and over-represented in the sample. Researchers must also be descriptive in the outcomes and effects of those participants that were left out and/or the participants that were overrepresented had on the researcher's results. This gives the audience a good idea of the sample size that the researcher tested and allows them to make a distinction between the researcher's results and the results from a random survey representative of the entire population.

Data Collection

A survey was administered to each of the participants. This survey asked a variety of questions from privacy to safety. The survey can be found in Appendix A. There were 21 different questions in this survey.

Variables

Dependent Variable: Whether implementing CCTV cameras in public areas will be effective in reducing, deterring and preventing crime.

Independent Variables:

Age: In years

Gender: Male, Female

Ethnicity: Mixture of ethnic backgrounds (e.g. White, Black, Hispanic, Asian, Native American Indian).

Degree Major: To determine if a student's educational degree has an effect on how they perceive the use CCTV cameras.

Results

Table 1 represents the demographics (gender, ethnicity, age and degree major) of undergraduate students that participated in this study. Of the 96 participants, 59 females participated in this survey representing (61.5 percent) of the sample size. There were 37 males that participated representing (38.5 percent) of the sample size. A total of 79 students were white (82.3 percent) and 17 students that were non-white (17.7 percent) of students. There are a variety of age groups ranging from 18 to 23 years and older in this study. There were 20-18 year olds, 34-19 year olds, 16-20 year olds, 6-21 year olds, 6-22 year olds and 14 participants that were 23 years of age or older.

Table 1

Demographics

	Frequency	Percent
Gender		
Female	59	61.5
Male	37	38.5
Total	96	100
Ethnicity		
White	79	82.3
Non-White	17	17.7
Total	96	100
Age		
18	20	20.8
19	34	35.4
20	16	16.7

21	6	6.3
22	6	6.3
23 & Older	14	14.5
Total	96	100

Table 2 lists the different degrees students were majoring in at Southern Oregon University. One participant majored in art, one participant was in business, five were majoring in communications (5.2 percent), three were majoring in computer science (3.1 percent), 43 students were majoring in various social sciences (44.8 percent), 16 were majoring in education (16.7 percent), one was majoring in engineering, two were majoring in international studies (2.1 percent), two were majoring in mathematics (2.1 percent), one majored in music, two were double majors, one was majoring in nursing, one was majoring in outdoor life adventures, one was majoring in product design, one was majoring in study arts, three were majoring in theater (3.1 percent) and ten had undeclared majors (10.4 percent).

Table2

Degree Major

	Frequency	Percent
Art	1	1
Business	1	1
Communications	5	5.2
Computer Science	3	3.1
Social Science's	43	44.8
Education	16	16.7
Engineering	1	1
International Studies	2	2.1
Mathematics	2	2.1
Music	1	1
Double Majors	2	2
Nursing	1	1

Outdoor Life Adventure	1	1
Product Design	1	1
Study Arts	1	1
Theater	3	3.1
Undeclared	10	10.4
Total	96	100

Table 3 addresses the question in the survey; "Should local authorities and the police use CCTV cameras to monitor public activity in towns and cities across the United States?" Five males said they did not know, 13 said no, and 19 said yes. There were 12 females who did not know, eight who said no and 39 said yes. All together there 17 answered did not know (17.7 percent), 21 answered no (21.9 percent) and 58 answered yes (60.4 percent). The majority of the participants believe that the police and local authorities should use CCTV cameras to monitor public activity across the United States. A large majority of females agreed while males were nearly split on the issue; a combined 18 did not know and no vs. 19 who answered yes.

Table 3

Should local authorities and the police use CCTV to monitor public activity in United States?

Gender	Don't Know	No	Yes	Total
Male	5	13	19	37
Female	12	8	39	59
Total	17	21	58	96
Percent	17.7	21.9	60.4	100

Table 4 addresses the question in the survey; "Are there too many, too few, or just the right amount of CCTV cameras monitoring public areas?" There were 18 males who did not know, 13 said too few and 6 said too many while 24 females said they did not know, 30 said too few and 5 said too many. All together there were 42 participants who said they did not know (43.7 percent), 43 said there were too few (44.8 percent) and 11 said too many (11.5 percent). It seems that the participants believe that there are not enough CCTV cameras monitoring public areas. However, when combining those who had no opinion (did not know) and the ones who thought there were too many, the results differ if one considers the answer "did not know" as being one of indifference. For example, 24 males vs. 13 who thought there were too few cameras and 29 females vs. 30 who thought there were not enough cameras.

Table 4

The right amount of CCTV cameras monitoring public areas?

Gender	Don't Know	Too Few	Too Many	Total
Male	18	13	6	37
Female	24	30	5	37
Total	42	43	11	96
Percent	43.7	44.8	11.5	100

Table 5 addresses the question from the survey; "Should authorities (police) restrict how many hours they monitor CCTV cameras to meet budget cuts?" There were 6 males who said they did not know, 16 said no and 15 said yes while 8 females said they did not know, 32 said no and 19 said yes. Overall, a total of 14 said they did not know (14.9 percent), 48 said no (50 percent) and 34 said yes (35.4 percent). The majority agreed that the authorities (police) should not restrict how many hours they monitor CCTV cameras to meet budget cuts. The male participants disagreed with their female counterparts in that the male no and yes answers were nearly tied.

Table 5

Should authorities restrict how many hours they monitor CCTV cameras for budget cuts?

Gender	Don't Know	No	Yes	Total

Male	6	16	15	37
Female	8	32	19	59
Total	14	48	34	96
Percent	14.6	50	35.4	100

Table 6 addresses the question; "If CCTV cameras were visible in public areas would crime increase, decrease or stay the same in CCTV communities if cameras were removed or monitoring hours were restricted?" 5 males said that it would decrease, 17 said crime would increase and 15 said it would stay the same, while 7 females said that crime would decrease, 34 said crime would increase and 18 said it would stay the same. Overall, 12 participants said that it would decrease (12 percent), 51 said that crime would increase (54 percent) and 18 said that it would stay the same (34 percent). The majority agreed that crime would increase if cameras were removed or monitoring time was restricted. Once again, the male participants disagreed with their female counterparts. A total of 20 males thought that crime would decrease or stay the same compared to the 17 that claimed crime would increase. Although, 25 females disagreed with their 34 counterparts who claimed that crime would increase. Overall, 46 percent believe that crime would decrease or stay the same compared to the 54 percent that claim crime would increase if cameras were removed or if monitoring hours were restricted.

Table 6

Would crime increase, decrease or stay the same if cameras were removed or monitoring hours were restricted?

Gender	Decrease	Increase	Stay Same	Total
Male	5	17	15	37
Female	7	34	18	59
Total	12	51	33	96
Percent	12	54	34	100

Table 7 addresses the question; "Do small and unidentifiable CCTV cameras pose a greater or lesser risk to personal privacy if they were used in public areas?" 6 males said they did not know, 19 said greater and 12 said a lesser risk to privacy while 10 females said they did not know, 31 said greater and 18 said a lesser risk to privacy. All together, there were 16 participants that said they did not know (16 percent), 50 said greater (52 percent) and 30 said a lesser risk (32 percent) to privacy. Over half the participants believe that small and unidentifiable CCTV cameras would negatively affect their personal privacy if used in public areas. If one considers the answer of "did not know" as being one of indifference and combined with those that answered that such cameras would be lesser of a risk to privacy then both the males and females are nearly tied with those that claimed that such cameras would pose a greater risk to privacy with those believing that it would be a greater risk to privacy holding the lead.

Table 7

Do small and unidentifiable CCTV cameras affecting personal privacy when used in public areas.

Gender	Don't Know	Greater	Lesser	Total
Male	6	19	12	37
Female	10	31	18	59
Total	16	50	30	96
Percent	16	52	32	100

Table 8 addresses the survey question; "If CCTV cameras were visible in public would this reduce crime?" 2 males said they did not know, 4 said no and 31 said yes while 6 females said they did not know, 3 said no and 50 said yes. Overall, 8 did not know (8.3 percent), 7 said no (7.3 percent) and 81 said yes (84.4 percent). The majority of the participants believe that if CCTV cameras were visible in public areas that it would reduce crime. The participant's answers were most likely based on their perception that the use of cameras would reduce crime, contrary to the results of some of the studies discussed above.

Table 8

If CCTV cameras were visible in public would this reduce crime?

Gender	Don't Know	No	Yes	Total
Male	2	4	31	37
Female	6	3	50	59
Total	8	7	81	96
Percent	8.3	7.3	84.4	100

Table 9 addresses the survey question; "If more CCTV cameras were visible to the public, would they feel safer?" 2 male participants said they did not know, 20 said no and 15 said yes while 12 females that said they did not know, 15 said no and 32 said yes to the question. Overall, 14 participants said they did not know (14.6 percent), 35 said no (36.5 percent) and 47 said yes (49 percent). Overwhelmingly, the majority of the participants believe that they would feel safer if there were more CCTV cameras in public. However, male participants disagreed with their female counterparts in that the majority of males answered no.

Table 9

If more cameras were visible to the public would they feel safer?

Gender	Don't Know	No	Yes	Total
Male	2	20	15	37
Female	12	15	32	59
Total	14	35	47	96
Percent	14.6	36.5	49	100

Discussion

There are several findings from this study. The results from this survey in terms of comparing it to the literature found that students who participated in this research seem to approve the use of CCTV cameras. The literature says that CCTV does not reduce, prevent or deter crime. The general student population at Southern Oregon University seems to like CCTV cameras. This also seems to coincide with some of the literature about the perceptions that some people have on CCTV cameras being implemented in the general public. This supports the hypothesis that even with mixed results from the literature, the general public seems to approve of the use of CCTV cameras.

The majority (60.4 percent) agreed that police and local authorities should use CCTV to monitor public activity. Only (44.8 percent) thought that there were too few cameras deployed. When it came to reducing the number of monitoring hours due to budget cuts, (50 percent) of those surveyed agreed that it would be unacceptable. The majority of those surveyed agreed that if cameras were removed crime would increase, but only by a slim margin of (54 percent). Another slim margin of agreement involved the use of small or unidentifiable (hidden) cameras; (52 percent) were concerned that it would affect their privacy. However, an overwhelming (84.4 percent) agreed that visible cameras would reduce crime, yet Table 9 indicates that only (49 percent) would feel safer if more cameras were visible which seems be a contradiction in terms.

Those that agreed that there is a need for more, visible cameras seem to contradict themselves since only (60.4 percent) agreed that police and local authorities should use CCTV to monitor public activity. Since there are contradictions in this survey, many of the students may have reached a point where they just did not care anymore and became lazy, did not fully understand the question or quickly skimmed over the question and circled an answer.

The main issue regarding the use of surveillance cameras seems to be the invasion of privacy. A large majority found it acceptable to use visible cameras but the use of small or unidentifiable (hidden) cameras was not acceptable. The majority of the sample population consisted of females. Since the majority of the sample population consisted of females, the use of CCTV cameras seems to agree with their responses. There has been research that has "consistently shown that females are more fearful of crime despite lower levels of victimization" (*12*). Females are more likely to be victims of crime than their male counterparts.

Limitations

This research has several limitations with one being this research was limited due to its small sample size of students that participated. The sample size could have been larger by going to more classrooms and administering the 21-question survey. More data could have been collected if there was ample time to survey more students. The students who participated in this research represent a small demographic profile of the local population. A larger sample population with a diverse crowd would have a positive effect on the results. Multiple colleges and surveying more students on Southern Oregon University campus could have diversified the demographics that represent the sample. This research would have benefited from more questions, specifically asking the students if they thought that CCTV cameras actually reduce and prevent crime. It could have also have benefited from putting an explanation on the survey of the Routine Activities Theory and how it relates to the use of CCTV cameras.

Policy Implications

Beyond crime prevention, deterrence and reduction, CCTV has also been and issue of many different policy and privacy implications. This goes beyond just looking at how CCTV is used in public places, but how it is being implemented inside schools in the United Kingdom.

Taylor (13) researched CCTV use in secondary schools in regards to privacy by addressing these five different factors: First, she studied the history of CCTV within the United Kingdom and how it was implemented inside the school system. Second, she looked at privacy issues, particularly the factors of time and place inside schools. Third, she questioned why privacy is so important and why it was at stake if CCTV continued to grow within schools. Fourth, she considered privacy as a human right and how it was defined under the laws of the United Kingdom. Fifth, she studied a recent study of three secondary schools in the United Kingdom and how the students felt about the use of CCTV within the school system (13). Many students thought that the placement of CCTV cameras within their school did indeed infringe upon their rights to privacy, particularly for the younger age group of individuals. In order to examine the problem of privacy, Taylor used four focus groups that were tape recorded to examine how each individual felt that CCTV cameras were an invasion of privacy (13).

There needs to be a re-evaluation of privacy laws that involve certain places such as bathrooms and locker rooms in schools where CCTV cameras are placed and used in order to prevent an infringement upon privacy. Furthermore, policy implications in the United States pose a significant constitutional crisis. Prior to 9/11/2001 there was little need to collect information. However, the event that took place on 9/11/2001 changed all that.

The increased use of surveillance cameras dramatically increased, yet studies have shown they do not enhance safety. Are tax dollars being wasted by the government by implementing spy technology that can intercept our e-mails and wiretap our phones us without a warrant?

This is creating the illusion of enhancing safety. Is the public letting its guard down under the perceived umbrella of safety by relying on CCTV cameras that make them feel safe? This is nothing more than a scenario created by the government to make Americans less fearful of crime. If only the government would stop and read the constitution and respect the limits it has set.

While CCTV cameras might show some reductions of specific crimes depending largely on how, where, and why they are used, the public seems to want CCTV in public places in order to prevent, deter and reduce crime. What the public disagrees with is the constant use of cameras on a 24-hour, seven days a week basis in regards to invasion of privacy. The public wants to feel safe, however little evidence is available that camera surveillance actually makes them safer. The public is either ignorant of or indifferent to the cost of what it takes to install, monitor and maintain these cameras and the constitutional aspects of such use.

In addition, one has to consider a person is required to maintain and monitor the cameras. Failure to do so, coupled with electrical failures, jeopardizes the effectiveness of the system. Some laws, regulations, rules and policies prohibit the storage of images for more than a few days or over a week.

Conclusion

In conclusion, it is apparent that the public finds the use of CCTV surveillance as being acceptable, yet it does not make them feel as safe as they would like. Apparently, the public does not trust the practice knowing that certain crimes will occur regardless if the cameras are in place or not.

If CCTV is going to be effective it must be implemented in the right location and at the right time where crime seems to be prevalent, but without violating an individual's constitutional right to privacy. It's most important use can be that of enhancing criminal investigations.

References

1. E. Taylor, "Evaluating cctv: why the findings are inconsistent, inconclusive and ultimately irrelevant. *Crime Prevention and Community Safety*. **12(4)**, 209-232 (2010). doi:10.1057/cpcs.2010.13.

2. L. E. Cohen, M. Felson, Social change and crime rate trends: a routine activity approach. *American Sociological Review*. **44(4)**, 588 (August, 1979).

3. J. M. Caplan, L.W. Kennedy, G. Petrossian, Police monitored cctv cameras in newark, nj: a quasi-experimental test of crime deterrence. *J Exp Criminol*. **7**, 255-274 (2011). doi:10.1007/s11292-011-9125-9.

4. D.P. Farrington M. Gill,S. J. Waples, J. Argomaniz, The effects of closed-circuit television on crime: meta-analysis of an english national quasi-experimental multi-site evaluation [Electronic version]. *J Exp Criminol*. **3**, 21-38 (February, 2007). doi:10.1007/s11292-007-9024-2.

5. C. Norris, M. McCahill, CCTV: beyond penal modernism. *Brit. j. Criminol*. **46**, 97-118 (2006). doi:10.1093/bjc/azi047.

6. S. Waples, M. Gill, The effectiveness of redeployable cctv. *Crime Prevention and Community Safety*, **8**, 1-16 (2006). doi:10:1057/palgrave.cpcs.8150003

7. S. Waiton, The politics of surveillance: big brother on prozac. *Surveillance and Society*. **8(1)**, 61-84 (2010).

8. G. G. Clavell, L. Z. Lojo, A. Romero CCTV in Spain: an empirical account of deployment of video surveillance in a southern-european country. *International Journal of Government and Democracy*. **17**, 57-68 (2012). doi:10.3233/IP-2011-0254.

9. N. Zurawski, From crime prevention to urban development. *The International Journal of Government and Democracy*. **12**, 45-55 (2012). doi:10.3233/IP-2011-0250.

10. C. Fonio, The silent growth of video surveillance in Italy. *The International Journal of Government and Democracy*. **16**, 379-388 (2012). doi:10.3233/IP-2011-0248.

11. M. L. Dantzker, R. D. Hunter, *Research methods for criminology and criminal justice* (Sudbury, MA: Jones & Bartlett Learning, LLC., ed. 3, 2012), pp. 74-116. [third edition]

12. R. R. Dobbs, C. A. Waid, T. O. Shelley, Explaining fear of crime as fear as rape among college females an examination of multiple campuses in the united states. *International Journal of Social Inquiry.* **2(2)**, 105-122 (2009).

13. E. I. Taylor, I spy with my little eye: the use of cctv in schools and the impact on privacy. *The Sociological Review.* **58(3)**, 381-402 (2010).

Appendix

Closed-circuit television cameras (CCTV) are used to monitor and record certain events that happen at specific locations and times. CCTV is used as an environmental tool in order to prevent, reduce and deter crime. The purpose of this survey is to try and find out if CCTV actually works at reducing, preventing and deterring crime.

Please take the time to finish this survey and double check to see if you have missed any questions. Thank you for your time and effort and I wish each of you to a bright and hopeful future.

Gender: (Please check one.)

　　　____Female
　　　____Male
　　　____Other

Ethnicity: (Please check one.)

　　　____White (Non Hispanic)
　　　____American Indian or Alaskan Native
　　　____Hispanic/Latin American
　　　____Black/African-American
　　　Other (Please Specify) _____

Age:_____

Degree Major:_____

Degree Minor:_____

PLEASE CIRCLE YOUR ANSWERS

1. Should local authorities and the police use CCTV cameras to monitor public activity in towns and cities across the United States?

Yes   No   I don't know

2. Do you think that there are too many, too few or the right amount of CCTV cameras monitoring public areas (e.g. parking lots,

Too many   Too few   I don't know

3. Should the authorities (police) remove public CCTV cameras to meet budget cuts?

Yes   No   I don't know

4. Should the authorities (police) restrict how many hours they monitor CCTV cameras to meet budget cuts?

Yes   No   I don't know

5. Would crime increase, decrease, stay the same in CCTV communities if cameras were removed or monitoring hours were restricted?

Increase   Decrease   Stay the same

6. Would you agree that if CCTV cameras were visible in public areas that this would reduce crime?

Yes   No   I don't know

7. Would having more CCTV cameras that were visible to the public make you feel safer?

Yes   No   I don't know

8. Would you agree that by having CCTV cameras monitoring in public areas that this would make police respond in a quick and expedient manner to catch criminals?

Yes   No   I don't know

9. With CCTV cameras installed in public areas, would this provide valuable evidence to the authorities in order to help solve criminal acts that have already been committed?

Yes   No   I don't know

10. Would you agree that CCTV cameras in public areas provides evidence of post criminal activity by identifying offenders and witnesses and would provide useful evidence in order to catch criminals?

    Yes   No   I don't know

11. With questions 8, 9 and 10 in mind, would you say that what is recorded on CCTV cameras would provide more guilty pleas in the court of law?

    Yes   No   I don't know

12. Would CCTV cameras save money (for taxpayers) as it would provide good evidence in the court of law for a guilty verdict?

    Yes   No   I don't know

13. Do you feel that CCTV cameras in public areas infringes upon your personal right to privacy?

    Yes   No   I don't know

14. Do you feel that CCTV cameras that are visible in private areas which are operated by private businesses pose a greater or lesser risk to your personal privacy than those that are operated (in public) by the authorities?

    Greater   Lesser   I don't know

15. Do you feel that small and unidentifiable CCTV cameras pose a greater or lesser risk to your personal privacy if they were used in public areas?

    Greater   Lesser   I don't know

16. Do you feel that license plate recognition systems pose a greater or lesser risk to your personal privacy other than CCTV cameras used by authorities?

    Greater   Lesser   I don't know

17. Do you think that private businesses and companies should use CCTV cameras in order to monitor activity during and after business hours?

    Yes   No   I don't know

18. Do you think that CCTV cameras should be used for traffic enforcement purposes?

    Yes   No   I don't know

19. Should more CCTV cameras be used instead of traffic enforcement (speed) vans in order to deter/reduce speeding?

    Yes   No   I don't know

20. Should CCTV cameras just be used for stop light photo traffic enforcement (e.g. speeding ticket vans and stop light cameras) on public roads?

    Yes   No   I don't know

21. Should CCTV be able to be used on private property unregulated?

    Yes   No   I don't know

Twenty-First Century Alice

Timothy Hill – Southern Oregon University

Classic children's literature is seldom seen as feminist treatise or psychoanalytical reference. Charles Lutwidge Dodgson's (Lewis Carrol) *Alice in Wonderland,* and *Through the Looking Glass,* however, offer abundant evidence for both. After defining psychoanalysis, this paper examines Carroll's texts, as well as other sources, including his own diaries and letters; seeking to understand and name his motivations, while concurrently defining feminist goals and proving that Alice is a strong feminist role model through documenting her maturation from lost little girl to queen.

A minimal acquaintance with psychoanalysis is necessary for understanding the thesis stated above, particularly as pertains to the drives, or motivations of the characters or of Alice. The definition of psychoanalysis is: 1. A method of mind investigation, and especially of the unconscious mind; 2. A therapy of neurosis inspired from the above method; 3. A new stand alone discipline based on the knowledge acquired from applying the investigation method and clinical experiences (*1*). To investigate a mind, a psychoanalyst would ask pointed questions of a subject lying on a couch, evaluating their answers while attempting to uncover subsurface thoughts. Obviously it is impossible to sit in a room with Dodgson analyzing him; nonetheless, it will be done through his texts, and other reputable sources. To reiterate, the primary goal is to find the unconscious drives behind the literary works.

It seems that authoring any children's literature sufficiently interesting and diverse would require strong imagination. One immediately obvious and principal reason for the development and subsequent strengthening of Dodgson's imagination was a common affliction: boredom. Dodgson's father, Charles senior, was a country pastor. Thus, the parsonage in which the family lived was quite secluded, and young Charles junior was forced turn to the local animals and bugs for friendship. Inventively, he turned them into the kings and queens of his mind, even going as far as giving earthworms partial pieces of pipe for weaponry should they choose to battle (*2*). It could be said that his childhood play made no mark on the man's unconscious, but Dodgson's endless list of actors from the natural world: Cheshire Cat, Rabbit, Lion and Unicorn, even Flamingoes starkly refute that thought as they project from the condensations of the author's boyhood dreams to the pages of his adult works. The connection is easily made then, and the reader can see that though Carroll strove to write literature for children and adults, subconsciously he employed his powerful imagination- mentally hearkening to his childhood days of exhaustive search for entertainment; during which anything and everything including animals and bugs became topsy-turvy and nonsensical.

Lurking beneath the surface and hungrily seeking exposure (in his writing at least) was another of Dodgson's inner strengths: Mathematics. While studying at Oxford College, he earned a Boulter scholarship and later obtained First Class Honors not only in Math, but also Classical Moderations. Social subjects interested him, and he even edited *College Rhymes*, a Christ Church (Oxford) paper (*2*). Writing took up much of his time, and Dodgson published everything from mathematical pamphlets to philosophical papers, at least one of which- "What the Tortoise Said to Achilles" offers a playful approach to the foundations of logic, and is taught and revered even today (*3*). In short, Dodgson fancied myriad jobs and diversions, ranging from Chess to Photography. Yet, the study and instruction of mathematics were his primary employment and focus, and Oxford history as well as the Lewis Carrol Society cite him as maintaining a mathematical lectureship at the college from 1855 to 1881.

Why is this important? Because mathematical themes are laced throughout *Alice in Wonderland* and *Through the Looking Glass*. Just why is *that* important? Well, only a career mathematician moonlighting as a children's author could weave so many numbers and so much logic through his books, and sustaining such an endeavor would no doubt require great skill. Was this intentional or not? Most likely, anyone asked would say yes, and some even say that the use of math in AIW and TLG was a disguised attempt at bashing "new" math but what if it wasn't? It is possible that Dodgson only intended wittiness, sought to warm the hearts of adults and children alike with utterances pertaining to what he loved most. So, while it is not unreasonable to say that Professor Dodgson consciously sought to employ innate mathematical strength in his literary production, it is also reasonable to assert that he *unconsciously* applied the same.

A final word on Mathematics employed by Dodgson in his writing answered by a hypothetic conjecture of his motivations now follows. Post researching Dodgson's use of mathematics in AIW and TLG, two examples stand out. The first is Alice's rapid reduction resulting from a drunk potion, then wondering if she'll just keep shrinking forever, or eventually disappear. The second is her inability to add correctly after returning to normal size. A consortium of online info via NPR, The NY Times, and New Scientist from i09.com states these as references to asymptotal graphing and failed attempts to count in changed base systems (*4*). Hence, it is reasonable to assume that these were simply examples of Professor Dodgson's mathematical prowess. However, it can also be said that Dodgson was not necessarily always extremely motivated toward new theory or proofs and could have been unconsciously "vindicating" his work ethic in math through literary endeavors. That assertion *may* seem a stretch. Reading the author's diary, however, resolves any doubt of his occasional mathematical struggles. In January 1855, Dodgson himself wrote of, "Trying a little mathematics unsuccessfully," and "No mathematics again today" as well as, "Meant to have begun work today, but fell to illumination instead" (*5*).

Now that Alice's shrinking is a topic of discussion, it seems appropriate to question why. Why was she threatened by diminishment so frequently in Wonderland? For that matter, why was her very life or, "existence" endangered continually throughout her adventures underground? Luckily, she never did lose her head, get trapped forever inside a house she'd grown too large for, or "Drink too much from a bottle marked poison" because a very valuable lesson stems from her survival. The lesson, outlined in Carole Rother's *Lewis Carroll's Lesson: Coping With Fears of Personal Destruction* is rich ground for psychoanalysis, and will therefore be brought to light now.

Conscious or unconscious, an obvious motivation for writing books for children is a love of, and care for children. Much has been said about Charles Dodgson's "love" and "care" for children, which will be discussed later, but for now let's focus on Carole Rother's explanation of Carrol's motive. According to Rother, *Alice in Wonderland* and *Through the Looking Glass* were written to help children cope with their fears of self-destruction (*6*). It seems that children need help coping with a very basic fear: that they will disappear, thus their physical selves will be annihilated and their physical beings destroyed. The shrinking and other aforementioned near-death experiences are meant to be viewed by children then, as examples of handling threats and scrapes with nonchalance; actually having fun while doing so. Rother's article quotes Bruno Bettelheim's statement regarding the role of the fairytale in the psychological growth of the child, "Observations of reality sometimes evoke anxieties in children beyond their coping ability, thus they need help in overcoming fear and gaining strength from them" (*6*).

Explained thusly, it makes a lot of sense that Dodgson would portray Alice in seemingly constant danger, yet always successfully surviving and thriving. In fact, if one were to read AIW and TLG straight through without stopping, they would find Alice progressing slowly in confidence and knowledge with each calamity she faces. She learns to handle the constant shrinking through finding the right mushrooms to eat, makes allies out of the Cheshire Cat and Caterpillar, talks back to mean queens, and in the end even becomes a queen herself. Any child could easily imagine themselves as Alice, comparing their own successes with hers while gaining a symbiate confidence with hers. The burning question now though, is why? What motivated Dodgson to try and help children conquer their fears?

It seems that Dodgson was introduced to death very early on in his life; in fact, before he was even born. His grandfather, Charles Dodgson, was a captain in the fourth dragoon guards, and was killed in action by rebels at only 32 years old. Sadly, this was just three years after the birth of his first son, also the same year his second son was born (7). Surely young Charlie heard all about his heroic forebear while growing up, which could have resulted in a heightened sense of loss, and fears of his own tragic end. His mother, Frances Jane, lived to be only 48 years old, and when she passed away her son was just 19 years old (7). The young man was closely acquainted with death, and needed to learn how to cope with it. What better way to do so than pondering how to help others, eventually deciding the best way would be through his novels- allegorically engendering strength through conquering opposition. Unconsciously, Dodgson helped himself while helping others; as he gracefully employed his power to cope with the ultimate form of diminishment- death.

Whatever the man's motivations were, it is clear that the reverend, professor, mathematician, children's author and photographer Charles Dodgson, (Lewis Carroll) possessed unmatched ability, and left behind great works. It is also clear that in those works, he intended to assist children in their growing up, to cope with their fears, and in a way, to come of age. Before moving on to feminism, we will now look at one final motivation of Carrol's - to help Alice Liddel through her journey to womanhood by offering her an "Allegory of Maturation".

The introduction to *The Annotated Alice* states that Dodgson's greatest joy was, "Entertaining little girls," therefore it is appropriate to assume that one of his favorite little girls- Alice Liddell should garner his help in her journey from girl to woman. Upon introduction, Alice is seen as a bewildered, small child; hapless victim of nearly everything she comes across in

Wonderland—her new surroundings. Being thrust into Wonderland is like being thrust into puberty, everything you knew before suddenly turned upside down by raging hormones. Yet, over time, she grows adept, coming to the point of confidently questioning people, interactions and surroundings. Soon, the young woman speaks of, "Beating time" (*5*) in answer to the mad hatter's endless riddling, learns to control growth and shrinking by ingesting mushrooms, (*5*) and knocking over jury-boxes before presenting evidence in lieu of, "Losing her head" (*5*). Pages quickly turn in anticipation of her next move, and one can easily see Alice herself reading away, confidence bolstered and dreaming of coming confrontations with parents, teachers and friends.

So, the allegory moves on, and by conclusion of *Through the Looking Glass*, Alice makes a full transition into a real queen (*5*). Well, a queen of children's literature anyhow. The concluding thoughts remember earlier, easier times for Dodgson and Liddell. Within his terminal poem, Dodgson recalls three children nestling near; pleased by the hearing of his simple tale, yet sadness looms and time long pales sunny skies. Alice has grown, yet still her memory haunts (*5*). Why did she turn away so eagerly, ready to run into womanhood? It is what it is. Time never stops ticking away, and many years have passed since 1862. Charles Lutwidge Dodgson knew this, and though it was hard letting go, unconsciously he knew there was no choice. Hence, he honored his friend Alice the best way he knew: by engendering strength and confidence through his words.

Though it can be said that Dodgson did much for Alice through sharing friendship, offering his advice, and then of course immortalizing her, there are some who say that he was not the good friend he seemed. One such person is Christina Rossetti, who may have been Lewis Carrol's first feminist critic. She knew Dodgson well enough to correspond regularly with him, and Christina and her family were the recipients of one of the first manuscripts of AIW. It is important to note that her brother was one Dante Gabriel Rossetti, a painter for whom she modeled, and with whose stereotypical limiting of women she did not agree. Her relationship with Dante paralleled hers with Dodgson; she asserted that he too limited women in his own thoughts, and in how he presented them. Rossetti claimed that Charles Dodgson preferred to detain an, "Ever-young prepubescent female in a static domain where childhoods dreams are twined in memory's mystic band" and that Alice in Wonderland was an, "Attempt to arrest the feminine in a dream child not as she is, but was when hope shone bright" (*8*).

Why that is important to this paper firstly, is because it is important to understand that *stereotypification* of women and their roles is completely divergent from the feminist theory to be expanded herein. Secondly, it is important to note that since initiation, women- scholars in particular have objected to Carrol's portrayal of Alice. Feminist theory seeks to reverse a pattern and history of not taking women seriously, which can become so deeply ingrained that it seems natural - a practice labeled by feminists as *misogyny* or focusing on men and not respecting women (*9*). Since at times, Carroll portrays Alice as quite weak, bewildered, and seemingly incapable, it makes sense that feminists would object. Those traits are in opposition to the idea that a feminist role model must be strong. However, interpreting through the lens of early feminist criticism, or *images of women*, it is possible to prove Alice a strong feminist role model indeed.

To do so, requires beginning at the beginning. Immediately after young Alice leaves the safety of her riverbank and sisters to follow the sharply-dressed white rabbit down his hole, she begins to fall. Not a little fall, but a long, long fall. So long, in fact that she wonders, "How many miles have I fallen? I must be getting near the centre of the earth!" Yet, rather than play victim, just falling aimlessly, heroic Alice decides to take stock of her surroundings, noticing shelves and cupboards; even pulling ORANGE MARMALADE from one- all the while plummeting, possibly to her death (*5*). Still, all she could talk about was how daring people would think her once she was home, and that now falling down the stairs would be nothing. What is this? Is she turning dire circumstance to her favor, fortuitously manipulating better fortunes while anticipating future brave braggings?

Upon realizing that she's shrunken and forgotten the little golden key to the garden door she so badly desires to open, (*5*) forlorn Alice begins to cry. Does that stop her? No. Instead, pulling her own bootstraps, the strong young lady entreats herself, "Come, there's no use crying like that!" and, "I advise you to leave off this minute!" So, she does leave off, en route to the strength and confidence needed for the next growth opportunity. It comes in the form of a potion bottle labeled, "Drink me" which she does (*5*). Immediately, Alice grew bigger, bigger, and bigger until just about too big for the little house where she'd been drinking. Now, smashed, trapped and bewildered all she could do was wait for help. Instead, came predators- Rabbit, Pat, and the little lizard, Bill. Shrewd Alice of course waited for the opportune moment, and grabbed for that Rabbit through the window, then for Pat. That time she missed, but certainly not when

Bill was sent down the chimney after her. BOOT! Up goes Bill, blasted out by Alice's giant foot, never to mess with *her* again. Finally, she takes their weapons, (pebbles transforming into cupcakes), shrinks, and escapes! Free from confinement and foiled attackers courageous Alice moves on (*5*).

And on, and on. Throughout the remainder of her adventures in *Wonderland* and *Through the Looking Glass*, young Alice continually faces dangers. Afeared always, she finds ways to avoid and overcome, with surprising courage, death by loss of head (*5*) , learns to row with porcupine needles , asserts her uniqueness to an indifferent Humpty-Dumpty, leaps the brook of adolescence into womanhood , eschewed by nothing- including her own queenly crown (*5*). So, it is possible now to see Alice completely differently. Once a helpless little girl; cannon fodder for those who claimed her to be stereotypically weak and unresourceful, Alice has proven herself instead to be a brave, resourceful, mature leader.

Speaking of queens, before concluding this work I offer one last look at Alice as a strong feminist role model to be extrapolated from Judith Little's 1976 article titled *Liberated Alice: Dodgson's Hero as Domestic Rebel* . All 17th century English women, especially mothers, were socially expected to be demure, beautiful, soft spoken, expert home-makers and not much more. According to Little, Dodgson was disgruntled by his mother's adherence to the, "Victorian Woman" ideal (*10*) and that he resented being removed from her, "Breast and lap" so she could fulfill the Victorian "Job Requirement" of pumping out babies. Frequently, women in this role became domestic tyrants, ranting and bullying in the home while perpetuating the Victorian Ideal outside of it. Little asserts these persons exemplified the mean queens in *Alice in Wonderland* and *Through the Looking Glass* (*10*).

Contrasting that ideal, and keeping with the thesis of this paper, is pubescent Alice who, Dodgson unconsciously cast to express a feminist view of his reservations about Victorian womanhood. Along her journey into maturity, Alice must face some, "disillusioning emblems of femininity" (*10*) like the uncontented mother Duchess in her kitchen; resolved to pepper things up and fling her baby to Alice, along with the Queen of hearts, whose "fits" are actually allegories of the labor pains Dodgson feared may one day kill his mother, and dear Alice. Continually seeking entry into the garden, (womanhood) Alice finally enters it, only to find an angry parody of womanhood there, the queen who this time is meant to represent a corrupt and distorted image of what she herself desires to be. Rambling through various adventures while simultaneously rejecting idealist motherhood fantasies, says Little, Alice finally becomes a queen- though rejecting associations of royalty with maternity; instead focusing on her new, "rule" (*10*) Before getting there of course, she must witness the battle between her "hero" the white night, and her "captor" the red night, who end up falling from their mounts side by side and shaking hands. Shockingly, Alice runs off because she wants to, "Be a queen" not a rescued maiden/eventual wife. So, Little cemented her point, and mine quite well. Again, it becomes easy to view Alice differently. This time though, she is the rejector of idealist Victorian womanhood, who chooses instead to blaze her own trail through *Wonderland*.

    Now that it's over, I offer thanks for the resultant journey engendered through researching Dodgson and his famous Alice. Though I definitely did come across myriad viewpoints and theses contrasting as well as supporting my own, not one was completely alike and for that I am grateful. Now, I hold my own unique knowledge, accompanied by proof of the stance I chose to take on the *Alice* books. Therefore, I entreat you, as reader and pupil, to not only savor your new knowledge, but to read on; critically forming your own view. Finally, for your reading pleasure, as Carroll closed *Through the Looking Glass;* I now do the same: with a poem.

Today I stand,
Here
And here only. A man who's seen Twenty-First Century Wonderland.
New
Knowledge warmly fills my mind and
Soul.
Alice for me, will never be the same.
Look!
I see them: Cheshire Cat, White Rabbit, Queen of Hearts; all waiting to tell,
CARROL! Past perceptions erased.
Enigma is cleared, and Alice, I fear; grows ever stronger my dear.

References

1. "What is psychoanalysis?" (Freudfile.org, 2013, http://www.freudfile.org/psychoanalysis/definition.html)
2. C. Doman, "What the tortoise said to achilles" (PhilosophyArchive.com, 2010, http://www.philosophyarchive.com/index.php?title=What_the_Tortoise_Said_to_Achilles)
3. E. Inglis-Arkel, "A math free guide to the math of Alice in Wonderland" (io9.com, 2012, http://io9.com/5907235/a-math+free-guide-to-the-math-of-alice-in-wonderland)
4. L. Carroll, *The Diaries of Lewis Carroll* (Oxford University Press, New York, 1954)
5. L. Carroll, *The Annotated Alice* (New American Library, New York, 1963)
6. C. Rother, Lewis Carroll's lesson: Coping with fears of personal destruction. *Pacific Coast Philology.* **19**. ½, 89-94 (1984)
7. S. D. Collingwood, *The Life and Letters of Lewis Carroll.* (The Century Company, New York, 1898)
8. C. U. Knoepflmacher, Avenging Alice: Christina Rossetti and Lewis Carroll. *Nineteenth Century Literature.* **41**. 3 299-328 (1986)
9. R. D. Parker, *How to Interpret Literature.* New York: (Oxford University Press, New York 2011)
10. J. Little. Liberated Alice: Dodgson's female hero as domestic rebel. *Women's Studies.* **3**.2 (1976)

The Significance of Porn and its Effect on Committed Relationships with a Focus on Heterosexual Couples and the Female Counterpart

Amy R. Foust - Southern Oregon University

Abstract

This paper analyzes some of the immediate and long-term effects of porn exposure within heterosexual relationships, especially those on the women in the relationship. I chose this topic because I, myself, am in a committed relationship and the topic interests me. Seven sources were compared and contrasted in an effort to compile known knowledge into a more thorough understanding of how viewing porn works within the confines of a committed relationship. The articles agree on some points and disagree on others. For the purpose of the paper as a whole, the Attorney General's Commission on Pornography's definition will be applied: pornography is defined as any "material predominantly sexually explicit and intended for purposes of sexual arousal" (1986, pp. 228-229). This definition is ambiguous; hence, it makes it hard to draw the line between what is pornography and what is not. Therefore, some of the authors of these studies will define pornography in their own terms. Many of the journals utilized an internet-based approach (convenience sample) while others conducted an experiment that calculated the short-term effects. The main shared focus of these articles is analyzing the psychological effect of partners' use of porn on the female in the relationship, which most studies agree are largely negative. However, many also present the facts of how different dynamics of relationships change with the use of porn. They also attempt to see how various factors of a relationship and the individual members of it may correlate with a different reaction to pornography usage.

Since its invention, many studies have been performed on pornography and its effects. Different experimenters have tried changing factors such as age, race, gender, religiosity, frequency of use, and type of pornography used within studies and experiments in order to get a better grasp on the phenomenon that is sweeping the nation. Indeed, America is the number one producer of pornographic videos and websites (in 2006 about 12 percent of all websites were pornography-related) and it is estimated that about 40 million Americans watch porn on a regular basis. This is in part because the internet provides accessibility, affordability, and anonymity. Similarly, the term "sex" was the most frequently searched word on the internet (2002), furthering the idea that people are interested and actively searching it out. This paper analyzes the effects of pornography use on women in heterosexual relationships by comparing and contrasting the finds of experts like Butler, Bridges, Lever, Dellner, Maddox, Zitzman, and Kenrick.

The majority of these experimenters including those of Butler, Lever, Zitzman, Kenrick, and Maddox, found extremely negative effects resulting from the use of porn in committed relationships. Overall, they report that women whose partners use porn feel fat, ugly, unwanted, degraded, cheated on, and terrible in general. Many use the words "betrayed," "cheating," and "affair." They report feeling less intimacy, less investment put into them and their relationship and sex life, misunderstood, less respect for their porn-using partner, no emotional involvement, and that they are living a lie when presenting themselves to the world as a happy and loving couple. Porn use was, in general, found detrimental to three specific areas: the relationship between the woman and her partner, the woman's view of her own worth and desirability, and the woman's view of the character and personal worth of her partner.

In Butler's study (*1*) 98 students from the University of North Dakota, all of which were in committed relationships, were separated into three groups. Group 1 viewed neutral images of people, group 2 viewed pornographic images, and group 3 viewed images of scenery. The hypothesis was that exposure to pornography would affect the relationship (though it did not specifically note how it would affect the relationship or in what direction). Immediately after viewing the images the participants answered questions regarding their sexual relationship and satisfaction. As a result, a strong positive correlation was found between exposure to pornography and higher levels of sexually aggressive attitudes, negative attitudes, male superiority complex, and sexual aggression. Also, more exposure to porn was found to result in a report of lower relationship satisfaction and males were found to fantasize more so of individuals other than their current partner. In a similar way, in Kenrick's study (*2*) 196 participants were showed a photograph of a nude female after being exposed to either a) abstract art, b) other average nudes, or c) photos from pornographic magazines. The results were that the nude model was judged as less attractive after the participants had been exposed to popular erotica. And males who found the Play-boy type centerfolds more pleasant rated themselves as less in love with their wives afterwards. Though these experiments did not delve deeply into the reaction of the women to the pornography, it helps to illustrate that some of the fears that women find themselves experiencing regarding pornography are not unprovoked.

Lever expands this topic with her survey (*3*) involving 8,376 adult participants in committed relationships who either used porn themselves or had a partner who used it. The findings were that, overall, women watch far less porn than men do. These women reported feeling objectified by and mistrustful of their partners' use of pornography. The women indicated that they have less "real" sex because of their partners' O.S.A. (online sexual activity) and men similarly reported less arousal by "real" sex because of their own O.S.A. Consequently it was found that partners of porn users become less sexually desiring and less frequently sexually intimate.

Differing from the other studies analyzed in this paper, Zitzman's (*4*) focused on a long-term study of 18 wives recruited by 3 licensed marriage and family therapists ranging in 6-28 years in practice. These wives were initially unaware of their partners' porn use and then discovered it. The discovery of their partners' porn use caused the development of an "attachment fault line" in the relationship and an estrangement between them and their husbands as a result of feeling emotionally and psychologically unsafe in the relationship. This distancing of the wives from their husbands emotionally, psychologically, and sexually was seen as their way of protecting themselves from who they now saw as an unreliable partner. It was found to cause global mistrust in all aspects of the relationships and the wives felt it caused the deterioration of their marital and family relationships. The deceit surrounding the pornography was reported as a significant reason for the wives' loss of trust and change in opinion of their husbands and, for some, the hiding of it was more devastating than the actual viewing of the porn. In some of the couples whose husbands disclosed their pornography use after years of hiding it before their wives' found it themselves, voluntary disclosure was found to slightly diminish the negative effects. Zitzman commented that:

> "Pornography use and deception together account for a psychosocial experience for wives that is emotionally intense and relationally and psychologically disruptive, disorienting, and destabilizing- a seismic psychological, relationship, and attachment trauma."(*4*)

And many wives report it being similar to a PTSD-type experience. As their husbands emotionally disengaged from their wives and indulged in extramarital fantasies, opting for personal physical gratification over marital intimacy, wives globally felt a breaking of marital vows, lowered self-esteem, little to no marital intimacy, and feelings of inadequacy. It was also found that males such as these who view porn become more accepting of actual infidelity.

Lastly, the study done by Maddox (5) involved 1,291 unmarried individuals in romantic relationships between 18-34 years of age. The goal was to examine measures in communication, relationship adjustment, commitment, sexual satisfaction, and infidelity in relation to porn use. Participants were placed into one of four categories depending on their frequency and style of use: No S.E.M. (sexually explicit material), S.E.M. alone only, S.E.M. together with partner only, or S.E.M. together and alone. Individuals in the No S.E.M. group reported higher relationship quality overall that those who viewed alone. The same group also reported significantly lower negative communication, higher levels of dedication and sexual satisfaction, and significantly higher relationship adjustment than those in the alone-only group. The individuals in the together-only group also reported higher levels of dedication and sexual satisfaction than the alone-only group. Surprisingly, the only difference between those who never viewed and those who viewed only with a partner is that those who never viewed had lower levels of infidelity. As far as infidelity goes, those in the No S.E.M. group were found to be 9.7% likely to cheat, those in the together-only group were found to be 18.2% likely, those in the alone-only group were found to be 19.4% likely, and those in the together and alone group were found to be a whopping 26.5% likely to cheat on their partner (5). On a side note, the experiment found that prolonged exposure to pornography is related to doubts about the value of marriage and a higher endorsement of non-monogamous relationships. The exposure also led men to misperceive what a typical naked body looks like. However, this study began to divulge how pornography, when used with a partner to enhance the relationship, has significantly less negative effects- our first glimpse into the not-so-negative side of pornography.

Turning the tables, Bridges' study (6) did not find a majority of negative response to porn from the women involved. The overall purpose was to determine how women in general view pornography and, unlike the rest of the findings, the slight majority of women in this study did not endorse the stereotypical negative views on pornography. It is important to note, however, that no women showed *positive* views on pornography, only *neutral* ones. Still, close to half of the women participating in the study were found to have many of the same negative feelings mentioned in the previous study: 26% saw it as an affair, 26% felt they lost their partner to a porn actress, 29% reported not feeling like a loving couple, 30% reported feeling like a sex object, 32% reported that it negatively affected their lovemaking, 34% reported lowered self-esteem, 37% felt they were not comparable to the porn actresses, 39% felt global negative effects on their relationship, 41% felt less attractive and desirable, and 42% felt insecure. Married women reported significantly more distress, and the group of women found most distressed of all were those whose partners reported the highest levels of porn use. Dellner's study (*7*) found many of the same results within his 393 participants in committed relationships and added that men who used pornography to "cope" were found to have more negatively impacted relationships than those who used pornography to "augment" or "enhance" their relationships, in which case the porn use was found to have a neutral effect. His study suggests that motivation for use may play an important role into how women feel about their partners' porn use.

In short, it is apparent that pornography does more harm than good. However, if the temptation is just too great, the healthiest way to partake is to use it sparingly, with a partner, as a tool for enhancing your relationship (*5*). The women in Lever's study suggest utilizing amateur pornography because it portrays "real women with real flaws"(*3*). If not careful pornography can cause detrimental effects to many aspect of one's relationship, especially the emotions of the female counterpart, evident throughout each of these studies. The findings of Zitzman's study urge us all to talk to our partners about pornography use and come up with a compromise that both parties are comfortable with. Honesty regarding pornography goes a long way. In the words of Zitzman,

> "Pornography invites and reinforces a non-intimate, non-relational, and therefore non-demanding sexual experience- a detached, disconnected physiological arousal suited to the self-engrossed preoccupation typical of addictive experience and escape"(*4*).

References

1. M. E. Butler, J. E. Holm, F. R. Ferraro, Pornography's immediate effect on relationship satisfaction. *Psi Chi Journal of Undergraduate Research.* **16.3**, 113-122 (2011).

2. D. T. Kenrick, S. E. Gutierres, L. L. Goldberg, Influence of popular erotica on judgments of strangers and mates. *Journal of experimental social psychology.* **25.2**, 159-167 (1989).

3. J. Lever, Perceived consequences of casual online sexual activities on heterosexual relationships: a U.S. online survey. *Archives of sexual behavior.* **40.2**, 429-439 (2011).

4. S. T. Zitzman, M. H. Butler, Wives' experience of husbands' pornography use and concomitant deception as an attachment threat in the adult pair-bond relationship. *Sexual Addiction & Compulsivity.* **16.3**, 210-240 (2009).

    A. M. Maddox, G. K. Rhoades, H. J. Markman, Viewing sexually-explicit materials alone or together: associations with relationship quality. *Archives of Sexual Behavior.* **40.2**, 441-448 (2011).

A. J. Bridges, R. M. Bergner, M. Hesson-McInnis, Romantic partners; use of pornography: its significance for women. *Journal of Sex & Marital Therapy.* **29.1**, 1-14 (2003).

5. D. K. Dellner, Pornography use, relationship functioning and sexual satisfaction: the mediating role of differentiation in committed relationships. *Dissertation Abstracts International.* **69** (2009).

6. K. T. Burton, The effect of men's use of pornography and depersonalized sexuality on women: a multiple case study with a narrative focus. *Dissertation Abstracts International.* **71** (2010).

www.ingramcontent.com/pod-product-compliance
Lightning Source LLC
Chambersburg PA
CBHW080823170526
45158CB00009B/2509